THE PLURALIST GAME

THE PLURALIST GAME

Pluralism, Liberalism, and the Moral Conscience

Francis Canavan

ROWMAN & LITTLEFIELD PUBLISHERS, INC.

ROWMAN & LITTLEFIELD PUBLISHERS, INC.

Published in the United States of America
by Rowman & Littlefield Publishers, Inc.
4720 Boston Way, Lanham, Maryland 20706

3 Henrietta Street
London WC2E 8LU, England

British Cataloging in Publication Information Available

Library of Congress Cataloging-in-Publication Data
Canavan, Francis
The pluralist game : pluralism, liberalism, and the moral
conscience / Francis Canavan.
p.   cm.
Includes index.
1. Political ethics.   2. Pluralism (Social sciences)
3. Liberalism.   I. Title.
JA79.C25   1995   172'.2—dc20   95-4609   CIP

ISBN 0–8476–8093–2 (cloth: alk paper)
ISBN 0–8476–8094–0 (pbk: alk paper)

Printed in the United States of America

 The paper used in this publication meets the minimum requirements of American National Standard for Information Sciences—Permanence of Paper for Printed Library Materials, ANSI Z39.48–1984.

To
William Bentley Ball
champion of genuine pluralism

Contents

Preface

This volume is a collection of articles that I wrote over a period of thirty years, from 1963 to 1993. They were not a planned series developing a single theme, nor were they by any means the only articles I wrote in those decades. They are simply those of my writings that in one way or another treated a subject that has long occupied my mind: the relationship among religion, morals, law, and public policy in a pluralistic liberal society. They are therefore "spotty" and do not form a complete treatment of the subject. Yet they do express a unified view of it, which I hope the reader will find to be at least provocative.

The articles are presented here in a roughly chronological order. I have pulled some of them out of that order, however, to put them next to articles dealing with similar topics. Thus, the first two introductory articles are followed by five on decisions of the U.S. Supreme Court and their effect on religion and morals in our country. The next four articles deal with pluralism and "the pluralist game," i.e., the way in which we attempt to resolve the problems arising out of our pluralism through the political, which includes the judicial, process. The following three articles criticize the corrosive effects of liberal individualism on our pluralistic society and its government. The last one defends the right of religious people, Catholics in particular, to participate fully in the political process, on those matters that are properly subject to that process, and not to be excluded on the ground that their consciences are formed by their religious beliefs. The sections of articles just mentioned, however, are not neatly and tightly divided; Supreme Court decisions, for example, are referred to in most of them.

I have edited the articles down, sometimes severely, in order to eliminate repetitions insofar as that has been possible. I have made no effort, however, to update the articles and make them refer to events and developments subsequent to the time when they were written. Each article speaks in the time in which it was originally written. But I have inserted references back to passages that appear earlier in this volume. The reason is usually because the reader will there find a full text of a passage that I had originally cited in this place but have eliminated to avoid repetition. Or it may be simply to make the reader aware that I know I am repeating myself.

I doubt if the reader will find any marked change in my thoughts on pluralism over the years. The chief one is a growing disillusionment with the pluralist game as actually played. "Law and Morals in a Pluralist Society" may strike the reader as naive; it so strikes me today. When I wrote it, I thought that we Americans were by and large honest and tolerant people who differed on certain important moral points, but who were open to reasonable accommodations. It gradually dawned on me that those with whom I differed were often intense partisans who believed, in the words of Vincent Lombardi of happy memory, that winning is the only thing. Yet I have not changed my mind on the main point of that article, that a country's laws will inevitably reflect the moral consensus of the people, and that in a pluralistic society, when we are acting for the preservation or the improvement of public morals, we must get an adequate degree of popular consent to our proposals.

In "Implications of the School Prayer and Bible Reading Decisions," I wrote: "Constitutional questions are answered ultimately by lawyers and judges. It is well that they are." I would no longer be so sure about that. But that article was written before *Griswold v. Connecticut,* which began the Court's discovery of an ever-expanding array of unspecified rights in "substantive due process." Later in the same article I wrote: "The welfare state is here and will get bigger rather than smaller as the years go by." To say that was understandable in 1964, but today the welfare state is in crisis in many countries, as well as in our own. I still think that it will necessarily remain in any developed economy, but not that it will get bigger.

I could mention other matters on which I have changed my mind, but fundamentally my views are the same. As the years have gone by, I have only become more convinced that a rights-based liberal individualism does not furnish us with adequate means for dealing with the problems of a pluralistic society, and that we, as a people, must seek a better intellectual and moral foundation for our polity. The prospects for success in that endeavor are not bright, but the thesis of this book is that we have no alternative.

I have dedicated the book to William Bentley Ball, an attorney who has appeared on numerous occasions before the U.S. Supreme Court to argue church-state cases. I know that, on certain points, Mr. Ball has not always agreed with me, nor I with him. But I dedicate the book to him out of sincere admiration for him as a courageous and untiring champion of genuine pluralism.

I owe a debt of gratitude to the Earhart Foundation for a generous grant to defray the expense of preparing this book for submission to the publisher. I also express my thanks to the several holders of the copyrights to the articles listed below. The only article contained in the book that is omitted from the list is "Government, Individualism, and Mediating Communities," which was published in a book now out of print, and whose copyright holder is no longer in operation. For the rest, permission to reprint has been obtained in each instance from the copyright holder.

"New Pluralism or Old Monism," *America* 109 (November 9, 1963): 556–60.

"Law and Morals in a Pluralist Society," *Pax Romana Journal,* no. 5 (1965): 3–6.

"Implications of the School Prayer and Bible Reading Decisions: The Welfare State," *Journal of Public Law* 13 (1965): 439–46.

"The Impact of Recent Supreme Court Decisions on Religion in the United States," *Journal of Church and State* 16 (1974): 217–36.

"The Girl in the Glass Box," *Human Life Review* 9, 1 (1983): 16–20.

"Natural Law and Judicial Review," *Public Affairs Quarterly* 7 (1993): 277–86.

"The Pluralist Game," *Law and Contemporary Problems* 44 (1981): 23–37.

"The Problem of Belief in America," *Communio* 2 (1975): 380–92.

"Our Pluralistic Society," *Communio* 9 (1982): 355–67.

"Unity in Diversity," *The World & I* 2, 9 (September 1987): 47–54.

"Liberalism in Root and Flower," in *The Ethical Dimension of Political Life,* ed. Francis Canavan (Durham, N.C.: Duke University Press, 1983): 40–48.

"Brief Essays on Liberalism and Liberty," from *Pins in the Liberal Balloon* (New York: National Committee of Catholic Laymen, 1990): 88, 106, 124, 148, 157.

"Political Choice and Catholic Conscience," in *When Conscience and Politics Meet,* no editor named (San Francisco: Ignatius Press, 1993): 47–58.

1

New Pluralism or Old Monism

The U.S. Supreme Court's decisions in the public school prayer and Bible-reading cases of 1962 and 1963 marked the end of an era of sacralism in America and the opening of a true age of pluralism. Unhappily, American Catholics are among those who are least ready to greet this new dawn of freedom. Such is the theme of an article that Daniel Callahan, associate editor of *Commonweal*, published in the September 6 issue of that journal under the title "The New Pluralism: From Nostalgia to Reality."

"The real confrontation with pluralism is only now beginning," says Mr. Callahan. He is chagrined to find his coreligionists reluctant to join in the confrontation because of their nostalgia for the vanished sacral order of society. At the same time, he offers little evidence that other groups in the population, or he himself, for that matter, are any better prepared to face the age of pluralism. If Mr. Callahan has a deeper understanding than other Catholics of what a pluralist society, as distinct from a merely secular one, may be, he keeps it hidden. The new pluralism, as he expounds it, looks like an old and tired secular monism.

It is not that one disagrees entirely with Mr. Callahan. In deciding the prayer cases, the Supreme Court has indeed put an end to an era in American education and in American life generally. The era is one whose passing we may mourn, but we should not let our tears blind us to the prospect opening before us. We are possibly—though only possibly—at the beginning of a new, more realistic, and, we may hope, more generous response to the fact of American pluralism.

Only, let us not deceive ourselves as to what the Supreme Court has accomplished with its prayer-case decisions. The Court's intention was

America (November 9, 1963)

1

to make the state neutral in religion. It has surely failed, however, to make the state neutral in education. All that the Court has done is to secularize the public school. It has not yet undertaken a real confrontation with pluralism, nor has the nation as a whole.

Ruling religion out of the public school is not an adequate answer to the problem of education in a pluralist society. It is rather an attempt to evade the question. A school that presumes to give children a complete formal education in a religiously neutral way has committed itself, as Honor Tracy might say, to walking the straight and narrow path between belief and unbelief. One may doubt whether the feat is any more possible than treading a line between right and wrong.

Public schools in the United States are not antireligious—far from it. But they are commanded by the Supreme Court to be nonreligious. Religious neutrality, it seems, consists in not saying anything for or against religion. Yet when the state teaches only secular subjects from a secular point of view in its schools, it willy-nilly favors those of its citizens who regard religion as irrelevant to life and believe that all human problems have purely human and secular answers. But there is nothing inherently secular about education. At least, there is nothing in the genius of a pluralist society that obliges us to believe in the natural secularity of education.

As for the Constitution of the United States, it simply forbids us to establish a religion. It does not command us to establish as our official educational philosophy a theory acceptable to the Ethical Culture Society.

We must recognize that the problem posed by the prayer cases is one that is inherent in the idea of public education. The root of the problem is the notion that the state must offer all its citizens a *common* education. That is why Protestants, when they set up the public school system in the nineteenth century, vetoed the teaching of sectarian doctrines on which they differed among themselves. Catholics then vetoed Protestantism; Jews vetoed Christianity; and secularists have now succeeded in vetoing religion altogether in public education. This was the inevitable result of trying to give a common education to a religiously divided society. The attempt tends necessarily to an education whose principles and values are wholly secular.

The Supreme Court has now accepted the argument that religion, as such, differentiates believers from unbelievers and therefore cannot be a part of the common education of children. But the Court has not yet questioned the twofold assumption that it is the state that educates, and that it must educate all children alike, without regard to the parents' deepest beliefs and educational preferences.

It is this largely unconscious and therefore uncriticized premise of the argument that we must bring out into the light and examine. In this connection, there are certain questions that it is almost impossible to get people in this country to think about seriously. They badly need discussing, however, if we are to face honestly the implications of a pluralist society where all beliefs stand on a plane of equality before the law.

1. Is the public school nothing but the state functioning as a teacher? The Supreme Court constantly makes that assumption; it is, indeed, the major premise of the Court's decisions in all cases involving religion in the public schools. Yet Americans more often than not think of the public school as a community school rather than as a state institution. In their minds, P.S. 3 belongs to the people of the neighborhood rather than to the state of New Jersey or of Oregon.

Surely it makes a difference which view we take. The state, we all agree, is secular; the promotion of religious faith is not its function. But the rules imposed on the state by its secularity are not the supreme law of society or of all the institutions of social welfare. For the community is not merely secular. Though divided in faith, the community is largely religious.

Seventy percent of the people questioned in a Gallup poll said that they disagreed with the Supreme Court's prayer and Bible-reading decision of last June 17. Public opinion polls do not decide questions of constitutional law, of course. But this one indicated that most Americans object to the total elimination of religion from the formal education of their children. If the school is an agency of the community, their wishes deserve some respect.

2. Is the state, which is the political organization of society, competent to educate? Do we accept it as having a mission to teach, and if so, what should it teach? What truth and wisdom does the state possess, that we should consider it peculiarly suited to instruct the minds and inspire the hearts of each new generation?

The Founding Fathers said in the Declaration of Independence: "We hold these truths to be self-evident, that all men are created equal, that they are endowed by their Creator with certain unalienable rights. . . ." Those words were written long ago, when the nation as a nation professed to believe certain truths about man and God. The Supreme Court would hardly tolerate their being taught to children in a public school today except as a piece of history. In the light of the Court's decisions, the truth is that the state now stands for no truths. The conclusion ought to be that the state is not well qualified for the task of teaching.

Granted, society has an enormous and growing stake in education, and it must act largely through the instrumentality of the state in order to finance and coordinate educational institutions. It does not follow that the state itself must act as a teaching institution. The function of the state is to see that all children are educated. A free society, however, can surely use other agencies than the state to do the educating.

3. If the state must conduct schools because voluntary, nonstate schools are unable to perform the whole task of education, does it follow that only state schools may receive public support? The public school is at present the dominant educational institution in this country. I, for one, foresee no future time in which it will occupy an inferior position. I am far more confident on that score than the people who insist that federal aid must be for public education alone. But I should think that if a private, nonprofit school gives a good general education, it serves the public interest and for that reason may receive public support.

Only a part of the public may want to send its children to that kind of school, especially if it is a denominational parochial school. But in a pluralist society, the public ought to give some measure of support to different kinds of schools, precisely as a recognition of pluralism.

4. In the public schools, which the state conducts, can only that limited kind of education be given that falls within the competence of the state? The state is secular; it therefore gives only secular instruction. But is the public school an agency of the state alone? Should we not regard it as also an agency of the community, which is a much deeper and richer reality than the state?

It is well known that many members of the community want their children to get religious instruction as part of their formal education. The state has no right to force such instruction on the children of those who do not want it. But it is hard to see why the state may not accommodate itself to the wishes of a respectable body of citizens and provide for religious instruction by private teachers within the structure of public education. In so doing, the state would not act beyond its educational competence but would rather acknowledge how limited that competence is.

These are, of course, old questions. They have been raised before, and the answers I have suggested have been so long rejected that the questions themselves now seem naive. But they still pose problems that a pluralist society has to face. By its decision on the prayer cases, the Supreme Court has forced us to see with new clarity the true nature of the answers that have in fact prevailed.

Now that the Lord's Prayer and the ten verses of the Bible, recited without comment, are out, the premises of public education would seem to be the following: the state is fully competent to educate; only the state's schools have a right to public support; and the state's schools must observe a neutrality that in practice is tantamount to an official agnosticism.

Behind these theses lies a tacit denial of the reality of pluralism and the assumption that the United States is a monistic, secular society. This assumption affects not only education but also the other social services that make up the modern welfare state.

A pluralist society would institutionalize its social services in such a way as to give its citizens freedom to choose according to their consciences among a variety of institutions in such fields as education; health; and the care of orphans, the disabled, and the aged. A monistic society, if it happens to be a liberal one, takes an ambivalent attitude. Liberal individualism prompts it to guarantee the citizen's right to follow his conscience, if he has the will and the means to do so. But monism dictates that there should be only one set of secular, officially neutral public institutions in all fields.

There are historical reasons why liberalism and secular monism have gone hand in hand. Liberalism was a revolt against an officially Christian established order of society. One of the main aims of the liberal program was to free the individual conscience from the teachings of Christianity and, for that purpose, to secularize public institutions. Liberals did not conceive, any more than the members of the old established churches did, of a state that would accept both the existence of different religious groups and their institutionalization for purposes of public welfare. For liberals, religious liberty and the secularization of society were one and the same thing.

Liberal secular monism achieved no more of a confrontation with pluralism than did the union of throne and altar or the confessional state. Its full significance was not apparent in the nineteenth century, when the state's chief contribution to social welfare was to keep taxes low so that citizens could look after their own needs and those of the deserving poor. The one great area of public welfare that the state arrogated to itself was education. This is why the school question was the heart of the church-state controversy.

In today's welfare state, if we wish to achieve a genuine pluralism, we must come to see that secular monism is increasingly out of date. A state that not only conducts schools but also administers a wide and growing range of other social services does not behave neutrally merely by keeping those services strictly secular. The welfare society can remain free only by developing a flexible relationship to the welfare state—one that permits and encourages private, including religious, institutions of welfare to serve the public as effectively as state institutions do.

There has been an enormous expansion of public social services in the past century. Because of this, the state tends to absorb the educational and welfare institutions of society. One need think only of the steadily growing percentage of American college students who attend tax-supported state universities. To counteract this tendency, the state has to take positive action in the opposite direction. That is, it must recognize, utilize, and, if need be, subsidize nonstate institutions that serve the needs and satisfy the preference of the diverse groups making up the pluralist society.

Religiously affiliated institutions, under such a policy, would have no special claim to favor. Their only right would be to receive the same treatment as other private institutions serving public needs. The purpose of public policy would not be to aid religious institutions in their religious capacity but to foster the freedom of citizens to satisfy their social needs according to their consciences. In some instances, at least, it would not be necessary to aid religious institutions directly. The G.I. Bill of Rights gave government aid directly to university students to use in universities of their choice, and this model could well be imitated in other areas.

This policy, in my opinion, would be a realistic and generous response to the fact of pluralism. I find no sign in Mr. Callahan's article that he feels the need for such a response: all he does is to urge Catholics to accept a secular society. We can hardly be content with that advice. A secular state, yes. But not a secular society.

The "desacralization" of the state and its institutions satisfies what Mr. Callahan calls "a large Jewish-secular minority (supported by many Protestants)." If the process stops there, we shall only have substituted an agnostic establishment for the vaguely Christian one that Mr. Callahan is so eager to renounce. I know that a number of Christians are talking today as if they were so afraid of being corrupted by the Emperor Constantine that they long for the return of the pagan Roman Empire—there are nostalgias and nostalgias. But the new pluralism demands something better.

Any society is, as such, one society and exists under one political form or state. But a pluralist society, as its name indicates, is one that also recognizes the plurality of creeds by which its members live. In the pluralist society, therefore, there must be a loosening of the joints between the state and the social services, among which education is one of the most important. In a pluralist society, the institutions of social welfare take their form, not from the unity of the state alone, but from the rich variety of the community.

President Kennedy remarked earlier this year that we must make the world safe for diversity. He was thinking of international affairs when he said that. But we could do worse than to take his thought as our starting point in the confrontation with pluralism which, as Mr. Callahan reminds us, is only now beginning here at home.

2

Law and Morals in a Pluralist Society

The Church today, as Karl Rahner reminds us, lives in a diaspora. Not only has the unity of religious faith that the Middle Ages knew vanished, but the unity of moral conviction that Western society enjoyed until recently is breaking down in several areas of behavior. The most important of these is the rules of conduct governing the transmission and preservation of human life. Divorce, contraception, and abortion are increasingly accepted practices in most of the nations of the West, though they are still resisted in varying degrees by Christians. One need not be excessively pessimistic to predict that euthanasia and homosexual relations will become the subject of acrimonious public debate within the lifetime of most of those who read this article. Since all of these matters are also the subjects of legal regulation, or even of outright legal prohibitions, they raise for Catholics, as for others, the question of the relation between law and morals. To what extent, and in what ways, should the state attempt, through its laws, to enforce moral standards upon the entire population? This question is posed, not in a society that is united in its fundamental religious and moral convictions, but in a mixed and divided society. This pluralist society is, moreover, one that is undergoing rapid change—not always for the better—in many ways. Today more than ever, therefore, it is impossible to regard law as a mere extension of morals, or to maintain that all that is immoral can and ought to be made illegal.

A Catholic attitude toward law and morals must be a carefully balanced and nuanced one. Without attempting to outline the proper stance for Catholics to take on all legal-moral questions in every country, this

Pax Romana Journal (1965)

article will try to set down some guidelines for Catholic participation in the framing of laws.

First, however, it is necessary to say clearly that even in a pluralist society there is a public morality. Divided though it be, the community is a community by virtue of what its members have in common. Among the things they hold in common are certain moral values and principles. The commonweal depends in large part precisely upon these common moral convictions. Without them, the community would degenerate to the level of imprisoned criminals who are held together only by the walls that surround them.

It cannot be said, either, that this morality represents nothing but the will of a majority imposed on the minority that may disagree with it. Despite the skepticism and doubt that characterize our age, most people probably would still agree with Professor Paul Weiss of Yale University when he says:

> A respect for the rights of minorities is but a respect for the individuals who form the minority. It means that they are to be acknowledged to have the same rights as those who form the majority. Plural marriages, incest, human sacrifice, free love are to be denied to the minority, not because they are not liked by the majority, but because it would be wrong for anyone to engage in them. The representatives elected by the majority ought to act representatively even for the minority, and therefore ought to urge only what all ought to accept.[1]

There is, therefore, a public morality that law can and does enforce. But from this point forward certain distinctions must be made. They are well grounded in the tradition of Catholic moral theology and are nothing new. Nonetheless, they need repetition.

First, the law commands and forbids for the sake of men's temporal, not of their eternal, welfare. Directly, at least, the law intends to promote the welfare of society, not the salvation of souls. It therefore punishes crimes against society, not sins against God.

Furthermore, the law issues its commands and prohibitions for the sake of the community's welfare, not for the purely private good of individuals. It may, of course, aid individuals directly, as it does through the variety of social welfare programs that are characteristic of the modern state. But it does even this for the general good of society rather than for the private welfare of individuals. Where the state legislates on moral matters, its intention is (or ought to be) to promote public morality and not to intrude into the individual's private and personal life.

Having said this, it seems necessary to acknowledge the truth of a statement made by Peregrine Worsthorne in the London *Daily Telegraph* last March 21. He said:

> It is almost impossible, in an organized society, to conceive of a private act which might not, in some circumstances, harm others in one way or another. Just as low standards in personal hygiene can endanger public health, so low standards in private morals can endanger public welfare. It seems to me wholly misleading, therefore, to try to draw any theoretical line beyond which the law may not trespass. All human activity, however private, can legitimately be the law's business.

Yet, as Mr. Worsthorne himself says, human activity does not legitimately become the law's business until it begins to affect other persons and thus to impinge upon a public concern. Not only that; even though an action is harmful in some way to the community, it should not be made a subject of legislation until it is or threatens to become substantially harmful. Not every minor social evil justifies legal regulation or prohibition.

The old saying, "You cannot legislate morality," is at best a half-truth. Every country has a multitude of laws that quite effectively prohibit evil deeds and encourage, or even command, good deeds. The law does require social virtue of citizens. But it should not impose a standard of virtue so high that it is unrealistic to expect the majority of men to observe it. The prohibition of all sale of alcoholic beverages in the United States during the 1920s was, no doubt, a "noble experiment"—or so it seemed to President Herbert Hoover—but it failed miserably. The prohibition laws were not obeyed because they asked more than the people thought it reasonable to ask or were willing to give. To escape Mr. Bumble's judgment that the law is an ass, therefore, legislators are well advised to aim at enforcing only that degree of good conduct that is necessary for the peace, good order, and well being of society.

The law may, because it must, tolerate some evils in the realm of moral conduct. If prohibition of a vice is likely to work greater harm to the community than toleration, or if a prohibition is such that it cannot be enforced, or if it brings the law into disrepute, then lawmakers will prudently refrain from imposing it by statute.

For law is essentially practical. Its purpose is to enhance the welfare of the community by promoting those human values for which society exists: and this is surely a moral purpose. But law can realize this purpose only by achieving practical results that in fact foster those values in the existing conditions of the community for which it is made. We cannot judge the desirability of a law merely by asking whether it enforces a sound moral principle.

Lawmakers must estimate as realistically as they can all of the consequences that a law will have in practice. Flat prohibition of a vice may effectively suppress it in one community. But in another situation it may lead to other and greater evils, such as corruption of the police and of party politicians. The party politics of more than one American city are financed by large contributions from professional gamblers—whose activities are banned by laws that are intended to save the citizens from the temptation to gamble.

It is therefore permissible—at times even advisable—for the law to regulate and control what it cannot effectively abolish. The British seek to keep the spread of narcotic drug addiction within bounds by taking the profit out of the drug traffic. They furnish drugs free of cost to licensed addicts. Their method of dealing with this problem may not be the ideal one. But it appears in a favorable light when contrasted with the results of American attempts to suppress the traffic in narcotics by prohibiting it altogether. Sometimes law achieves better results when it works by indirection rather than by a frontal assault on an evil.

Nevertheless, law does have a legitimate function in protecting and promoting public morals. In performing this function, it reflects the community's moral conscience. For this reason, laws that impose moral standards on personal conduct ought to enjoy the support of a consensus.

A bare majority suffices to enact a tax law or to pass a measure for constructing highways. Such decisions, once made, are usually accepted by the defeated minority with more or less good grace. But a law that seeks to establish a moral standard of conduct cannot be enforced if it is not supported by the moral beliefs of the larger and sounder part of the community. This is what is meant here by the consensus by which laws for the protection of public morals must be supported. It is not unanimity. But it is a measure of agreement great enough that one can say, in a meaningful sense, that the laws represent the conscience of the community and do not merely impose the moral judgment of one part of it on the rest.

Moral-legal questions become acute, however, precisely when the consensus either does not exist or is called into question by a sizeable minority that is intent on changing the law. Here it becomes necessary to distinguish two "moments" in a changing society.

The first moment is one in which a new and higher moral standard is being advocated, with a view to embodying it in law. For those who accept Catholic morality as valid, such a situation is a rare one in modern societies. The tide is not flowing in favor of traditional Christian morality; the sound we hear today is the melancholy, long, withdrawing roar of the sea of faith. But if the tide turns—as tides do—then it will become relevant to make a suggestion: Catholics should be hesitant to enact laws that impose higher than the generally accepted standards of public morality. This is not to say that the law may never be made more strict. But it would be both wise and just first to convert society to our moral beliefs, and to achieve an adequate degree of popular consent, before translating improved moral standards into legal norms.

The more relevant question today, however, is how we should act in the other "moment." That is, in a situation in which a moral consensus that once existed, and which supported laws that are still on the statute books, is breaking down. This is the prevailing situation in most parts of what once was Christendom. The demand that is being pressed in the public forum on most countries is not for laws that more closely conform to the Christian conscience. Quite the opposite; the cry is for easier divorce, easier abortion, and the active promotion of contraception as a governmental policy.

In these circumstances, it is certainly not obligatory to capitulate at once to every demand for more "liberal" laws. Initially at least, the presumption favors retention of the existing law and the burden of proof falls on those who advocate change, not on those who oppose it. Law, after all, has an important educational function: it proclaims a public moral standard, and this is weakened when laws are changed in the direction of greater laxity. This is not a conclusive argument against any and all change in the law, but it indicates that a certain conservatism in regard to the law is also a part of civil wisdom.

The change of law on a subject of public morality is all too often taken by a part of the population as a modification of morality itself. The experience of some Scandinavian and Eastern European countries, for example, suggests that a "liberal" and "rational" legal attitude toward abortion convinces many people that they have a right to abortion. When even the liberalized law denies them a legal abortion, they resort to illegal abortion. The result is an increase in the number, not only of legal abortions, but of illegal ones as well.

One might fear with equally good reason that a completely rationalistic and utilitarian approach to divorce would only lead to more divorces rather than to divorces granted on more realistic and rational grounds.

Catholics could in conscience consent to a reformation of the divorce laws in many countries, even to a fairly drastic restructuring of these laws, if there were solid grounds for expecting that the general effect would be to promote the stability of marriage and to grant divorces only in the more extreme cases. But mere "liberalization" is hardly likely to produce such happy results.

There are sound reasons, therefore, for resisting the lowering of legal moral standards. Nonetheless, the law must in the long run reflect the beliefs of the people, because it ultimately depends on their consent. When the moral consensus that has supported a law in the past breaks down to a sufficient degree, the law must change or become a dead letter.

This has clearly happened, in the opinion of this writer, to the laws prohibiting the sale and dissemination of contraceptives in some states of the United States. These laws were enacted in the nineteenth or early twentieth centuries and reflected the prevailing moral convictions of what was still a predominantly Protestant America. Today they are kept on the statute books—though they are seldom enforced—mainly because the Catholic Church has opposed their repeal or "liberalization."

Since these laws were passed, of course, the Protestant churches have almost completely reversed their position on contraception. The anti-contraception laws thus no longer enjoy the consent of the community as a whole nor even of its largest part. That is sufficient reason for Catholics to agree to a change in these laws. The archbishop of Boston, Richard Cardinal Cushing, has in fact recently stated that he would not oppose an amendment of the "birth-control" law of Massachusetts (a state that has a slight majority of Catholics in its population), if safeguards against the sale of contraceptives to minors were included in it.

Since the anticontraceptive laws in the United States are largely dead letters, the issue that they raise is not a very practical one in any case. A much more urgent question is posed by the campaign that Planned Parenthood is now waging (with considerable success) to get municipal and county governments to furnish contraceptive services free of cost to the poor.

Since the community today, by and large, does not regard contraception as immoral, it is difficult to raise an effective public objection to a contraceptive program on the ground of its immorality. Such an objection is bound to be interpreted as an effort by one part of the community to impose its peculiar conscience on everyone else. It would seem to be a sounder position today to agree that the government may furnish what are now regarded as normal contraceptive services to married persons who are too poor to pay for them and who want them. We may insist that the agencies of government should refrain from coercing or pressuring or influencing the poor to practice contraception. For if the government should undertake to promote contraception, it (1) would make a public policy of a practice to which a significant part of the public still objects on moral grounds and (2) would adopt an attitude toward the poor that the middle class would never tolerate being taken toward itself: government interference in decisions about family size.

The policy of government neutrality in regard to contraception (neither denying it to those who want it nor promoting it as a public program) is obviously a compromise policy whose justification is the divided state of public opinion on a moral question. It is not wholly realistic, either, since government involvement in contraceptive programs inevitably means some degree of public promotion of contraception as a practice.

But from another point of view, this policy may be the only one that Catholics today can realistically propose in many communities. The law sooner or later will reflect public opinion. Attempts to prevent it indefinitely from doing so will only fail. There comes a time when honorable compromise may produce a situation that is morally more acceptable than the one that would be imposed by a victorious adversary. Surely aggressive public promotion of contraception is a greater evil than a relatively neutral governmental attitude toward it.

Since the law sooner or later must reflect public opinion, the mission of Catholics in debates about public morality is not adequately defined as one of advocating or defending laws that embody sound moral principles. In the long run, it is far more important to influence the public conscience from which laws spring.

Let us not deceive ourselves: this is not an easy thing to do. In a religiously divided and partly de-Christianized society, we cannot appeal to the authority of the Church or of God Himself. This is not to say that we should disguise the religious source of our moral convictions or pretend that we believe in the viability of a purely secular morality. But to achieve a consensus in the public forum, we must speak of fundamental human values that all can recognize and accept.

Even this is not easy to do in terms that will carry conviction to most people today. Modern man tends to be not only a skeptic in religion, but also an empiricist in philosophy and therefore a relativist in morals. The public moral philosophy of the West is turning into a secular utilitarianism that has little room for such ideas as the indissolubility of marriage, the sanctity of embryonic life, or the integrity of the marital act.

It is to men infected with this mentality that we must address ourselves. There is little use in asking them to impose on themselves laws that enact all of the absolute prohibitions and commands of Catholic morality. Nor would it be wise to seek this even if it could be obtained: God requires far more of us than human law can dare demand.

But we can hope, and certainly should try, to restore to the men of today an insight that they are losing: the Catholic vision that life is good and is a great gift from God. Because life is good, marriage is good, procreation is good, and the life that is procreated is good.

All that attacks or corrupts life and all that weakens the institutions that shelter and foster life, is evil. Only when modern men regain this vision can we stem the tide of opinion that is now undermining Christian morality and is therefore sweeping away the legal structures inspired by that morality.

As the British writer Norman St. John-Stevas says, in "democratic pluralist societies, social policies with moral implications are not laid by *fiat* from above but are evolved gradually through the rational reflections of free men."[2] Controversial issues are resolved not by plebiscite but by the graduate crystallization of public opinion—and this requires rational discourse that involves all citizens and all private institutions.

There is no guarantee, of course, that Christian morality will again prevail if only we faithfully play our part in the democratic process. But, as Hamlet said, "the play's the thing wherein we'll catch the conscience of the king." Today, the king is the sovereign people, and the only play by which his conscience can be touched is the free play of opinion in public debate. There is the stage on which Catholic citizens must perform their role in establishing a sound relationship between law and morals.

Notes

1. *Our Public Life* (Bloomington: Indiana University Press, 1959), 137.
2. *Life, Death and the Law* (New York: Meridian Books, 1961), 43.

3

Implications of the School Prayer and Bible Reading Decisions: The Welfare State

The simplest answer to an inquiry into the theological implications of the Supreme Court's School Prayer and Bible Reading decisions is that there are no such implications. The First Amendment is not a theological proposition. Decisions interpreting the amendment answer questions in constitutional law, not in theology. In the cases we are considering, the Court did not tell us what is true in religion but what is the meaning of the legal phrase: ''an establishment of religion.''

Yet although this is and will remain a question in constitutional law, it cannot be answered adequately in legal terms alone. The great clauses of the Constitution are too broad and too vague, yet too charged with significance for our national life, to be treated as if their meaning were comparable to the definition of a tort or a misdemeanor. Constitutional questions are answered ultimately by lawyers and judges. It is well that they are. But the Constitution does not really determine the answers that the lawyers and the judges give. What they decide depends upon the answers to deeper questions in our political and social philosophy. In the cases we are here considering, one must add that the decisions of the Supreme Court have reflected a philosophy of education as well. It is a naive view of the First Amendment that would hold that the establishment clause, taken by itself, compelled the Court to arrive at its decisions in the School Prayer[1] and Bible Reading[2] cases.

The Court could have recognized, for example, that the American

Journal of Public Law (1965)

public school is by its nature a compromise institution. Set up to serve everyone, the school cannot fully please anyone. Should it attempt to do so, it would be destroying itself. As the late Justice Robert H. Jackson warned in his concurring opinion in Illinois ex rel. *McCollum v. Board of Education*,[3] "If we are to eliminate everything that is objectionable to any of these warring sects or inconsistent with any of their doctrines, we will leave public education in shreds."[4] Had the Court chosen to heed this warning, it could easily have found the minimal religious observances contested in *Engel v. Vitale*[5] and in *School District v. Schempp* and *Murray v. Curlett*[6] were not an establishment of religion in the constitutional sense. There was nothing in the Constitution to force the Court to decide otherwise.

The Court made its decision, however, and it will not reverse it. The settlement of the School Prayer and Bible Reading cases marked the end of a line along which we will not travel again. However the American people may ultimately relate religion and education, they will not do it by incorporating religious practices or instruction into the common program offered to all children in public schools. They may try "teaching about religion"—though some of us would think this no answer at all to the problem—but public schools will not be able to teach religion as such to all pupils alike.

Attempts, such as the Becker Amendment,[7] to turn back the clock are worse than futile. They miss the true significance of the Supreme Court's decisions. It did not consist of banning prayers, still less God, from public schools. The important thing that the Court did was to determine the educational philosophy under which those schools must operate. Restoring a brief prayer and ten verses of the Bible, read without comment, will not seriously affect that philosophy.

The true premise of the Court's argument was the proposition that in a public school the *state* offers *all* children a *common* education. In a religiously divided society, such an education tends inexorably toward agnosticism in belief and secular utilitarianism in morals. It would have been possible, as was said above, for the Court to refuse to impose that conclusion on the nation's public schools by not finding it implicit in the establishment clause. But once the Court accepted the premise that it is the state that is the educator in public schools and that the state, being secular, must be neutral as between religious belief and unbelief, it could not do otherwise than it did in the School Prayer and Bible Reading decisions.

The Court's intention was to make the state neutral in religion. It did not succeed, however, in making the state neutral in education. The separation of religion and education does not make schools religiously neutral. It only imposes a particular educational philosophy on the public schools, one that is most acceptable to people who consider religion irrelevant to life. Because of the monopoly of public funds enjoyed by these schools, it confers on that philosophy the status and the privileges of an established doctrine.

The first question to be faced, therefore, is whether the First Amendment establishes a particular view of life and a corresponding philosophy of education. There are those who seem to think that it should. For example, Frederick C. Neff wrote some years ago:

> The problem of choice between secular and other kinds of education is not a matter of choosing between the moral and the non-moral. Rather, it involves a choice between two competing standards of the good life. In precise terms, the choice is between intelligence and dogma, between experience and speculation, between the demonstrable and the mystical, between diversity and uniformity; it is a choice between standards that are flexible and standards that are rigid, between methods that are critical and methods that are premised. A basic issue confronting the free, public, secular school of our time has to do with the moral struggle between freedom and the hostile remnants of a prescientific and predemocratic past. It is the issue of democracy versus absolutism.[8]

Mr. Neff's views are easily recognizable as the prejudices of the Enlightenment erected into a theory of education. What concerns us at the moment, however, is not whether Neff's theory is a true one; everyone is free to hold his own opinion on that. The question is simply whether this theory is established as an official orthodoxy that alone enjoys support by taxes and that alone is offered to children in the public educational system.

The Supreme Court has not gone that far. Its understanding of the premise of public education was expressed in the following passage from Justice Robert Jackson's dissenting opinion in *Everson v. Board of Education*.[9] (The italicized sentences were cited with approval by Justice Tom Clark in the majority opinion that decided last year's School Prayer and Bible Reading cases.)

> Our public school, if not a product of Protestantism, at least is more consistent with it than with the Catholic culture and scheme of values. It is a relatively recent development dating from about 1840. *It is organized on the premise that secular education can be isolated from all religious teaching so that the school can inculcate all needed temporal knowledge*

and also maintain a strict and lofty neutrality as to religion. The assump-
tion is that after the individual has been instructed in worldly wisdom he
will be better fitted to choose his religion. Whether such a disjunction is
possible, and if possible whether it is wise, are questions I need not try to
answer.[10]

One could speculate on why Justice Jackson did not need to try to
answer questions so obviously interesting and important, and why Justice Clark preferred not even to raise them. One might also wonder
what idea of the equality of all religions before the law underlies the
assumption "that after the individual has been instructed in worldly
wisdom he will be better fitted to choose his religion." However conge-
nial that assumption may be to the more individualistic varieties of Protestantism, it is hardly what Orthodox Jews, Roman Catholics, or members of the Eastern Orthodox churches have in mind when they send
their children to public schools.

But these speculations, though intriguing, are not immediately to the
point here. Emphasis must fall on the Court's assumption that secular
education can be so isolated from all religious teaching that the public
school can teach from no ultimate point of view at all. Underlying this
premise is a concept of education that identifies it with "all needed
temporal knowledge" and nothing more.

This theory of education makes sense only on the assumption, natural
enough in a frontier society, that education is given in a little red school-
house and consists wholly of teaching the "three Rs" and similar
purely technical subjects. For clearly, once teaching goes beyond tech-
nique and aims at imparting wisdom and understanding, it must speak
from some standpoint. Whether this ultimate ground is religious and
supernatural or secular and naturalistic does not matter. What counts is
that it represents an opinion in the realm of belief. As such, it is an
abandonment of the "strict and lofty neutrality as to religion" that the
Court takes to be the premise of public education.

The question, in other words, is this: Is a complete formal education
possible if it implies no ultimate beliefs at all? Alexander Meiklejohn,
for one, thought not. "The city of New York, or San Francisco, or Mid-
dletown," he said, "has schools whose task it is to prepare young people for living. What do those cities believe about living? What lessons
do they teach? Does New York believe anything? Has it any values or
convictions out of which a scheme of teaching may be made?"[11] As is
well known, Dr. Meiklejohn advocated the adoption of a "civil religion" à la Jean-Jacques Rousseau to furnish the necessary intellectual

base for public education. There is little danger that the Supreme Court would openly sanction such a step. But whether it is not implicit in any scheme of secular education that pretends to be more than technical training is a question that has to be discussed. We cannot simply beg the question, as the Court has done.

On our idea of what education is, of what its premises are, and of what it is supposed to do for pupils will depend upon our answer to the further question: Is the state competent to educate? The state can teach the "three Rs" and other technical subjects. But, if education implies the option in the realm of belief described above, such teaching is not all that is meant by education. To that extent, the state is not competent to educate.

The very effort to remain neutral while educating forces the state to adopt an agnostic position in regard to ultimate truths. But agnosticism is not an escape from doctrine. On the contrary, it is only one of several possible doctrinal positions, no worse than others in the eyes of the law, but no better either. "Neither [a state nor the federal government] can constitutionally pass laws nor impose requirements which aid all religions as against nonbelievers, and neither can aid those religions based on a belief in the existence of God as against those religions founded on different beliefs," the Supreme Court has said.[12] But that proposition is reversible. The state cannot pass laws or impose requirements that aid nonbelievers as against religion or that aid religions that are not based on a belief in God as against those that are. Therefore, precisely because it is religiously neutral, the state is not really capable of acting as an educational institution.

To suggest that education extends beyond the competence of the state, however, is not to urge the state to get out of the business of education. In this country, as in every other modern nation, the state is in the business so deeply that it cannot get out of it. The education of the young is a basic need of modern society. No agency other than the state can effectively see to it that all of a nation's youth are adequately educated. That the state has a major and unescapable role to play in education is therefore undeniable.

We must still ask whether the public school is simply an agency of the state, bound by all the restrictions imposed on the state by its secularity. Traditionally, Americans have thought of the public school rather as the people's, or the community's, school. The notion that the school was the state functioning as the teacher of the community's children and that the children were *élèves de la patrie* was looked upon as an alien idea—Napoleonic rather than American.

But the premise of the Supreme Court's decisions in all cases concerning religion and public education has been precisely that the public school is an agency of the state. What the state cannot do, according to the Court, the school cannot do either, because the school is the state in action. The state has no religion. The school, therefore, not only has no religion, but also cannot make a place for religion in its curriculum. It cannot do this even for those who want it and even when private persons rather than public school teachers are allowed to use public school classrooms for religious instruction on a voluntary basis.

This conclusion, at which the Court arrived in the *McCollum* case, deserves critical examination; so does the assumption behind it. Is education, when carried on in a public school, wholly a state activity? Or is it an activity that has dimensions that go beyond the competence of the state and which the state may allow pupils to reach by cooperating with other agencies whose competence in this respect is larger than the state's?

We thus come to the final and most important question: To whom does the school belong? The answer already suggested here is that the school belongs to the community rather than to the state. It is the state's right and duty to support schools, to coordinate them in a general system of education, to set standards for them, and even to establish them where necessary. But if the school belongs to the community rather than to the state, then the school should express what the community stands for rather than merely what the state is capable of doing.

It is the community, not the state, that has a spiritual, cultural, and intellectual tradition to pass on. The community has moral, philosophical, and religious beliefs, even if the state does not. The state, as an instrument of society, has a limited function. But society must support and foster all human values and must design the education it gives to its children accordingly. No school, of course, is a complete microcosm of human society, and there will always be "an awful lot of knowledge that isn't taught at Siwash College," to say nothing of P.S. 3. But the school, as an agency of the community rather than the state, can undertake to form children in all of the major values of society.

The community, however, is divided. It has moral, philosophical, and religious beliefs, but they are not the same beliefs for all groups within the community. It is this fact, the fact of cultural and religious pluralism, that makes the problem of publicly supported education so delicate and so difficult in this country.

As was said earlier, the effort to have the common or public schools transmit a minimal and supposedly common core or religious belief was terminated by the School Prayer and Bible Reading decisions and will not be revived. Two other courses of action, however, remain open and deserve brief mention.

One is to reverse the *McCollum* decision of 1948. That would allow public school pupils to receive some measure of religious instruction in public school classrooms and on public school time. Attendance would be voluntary and the teachers would not be public employees. Since the community is religiously divided, it cannot teach religion through its agency, the public school. But since the community, though divided, is still in large part religious, it surely can accede to the wish of a respectable part of its members that their children should get religious instruction as part of their education. Many people would not consider this arrangement as constituting an adequate and satisfactory relationship between religion and education. But it would at least be an acknowledgment by the community that education, in the minds of many citizens, includes more than either the state or the public school as such is competent to give.

The other course that is open to us is to give some measure of public support to nonpublic schools. The justification for this would be that, although they teach from a definite (usually religious) point of view, these schools nonetheless give a general education that meets the state's requirements. They therefore perform a public service and merit public support.

The constitutional principle that can be advanced to justify such support is found in the 1963 *Schempp* decision. The opinion of the Court, delivered by Justice Clark, laid down a test for the constitutionality of a legislative measure under the First Amendment's establishment clause in these terms:

> The test may be stated as follows: what are the purpose and the primary effect of the enactment? If either is the advancement or inhibition of religion then the enactment exceeds the scope of legislative power as circumscribed by the Constitution. That is to say that to withstand the strictures of the Establishment Clause there must be a secular legislative purpose and a primary effect that neither advances nor inhibits religion.[13]

The argument, under this test, for the constitutionality of public support of nonpublic schools with a religious orientation would run thus: The *primary* purpose and effect of the aid are to promote education in the service of the community. The aid to religion, that will admittedly also result, is secondary.

It is not this writer's intention to engage in a constitutional argument, however. Rather he would stress the point made at the beginning of this paper: The answers to constitutional questions depend on the answers to questions in social and political philosophy. If we think of ourselves as a society that is in fact religiously divided but aims to give the broadest possible measure of religious freedom, then we may ask what interpretation of the Constitution best accomplishes that end.

Behind all the discussion about religion and education lies our conception of a much larger reality than the school. It is our idea of the welfare state. It is increasingly obvious to all but the willfully blind that the question, whether we shall have a welfare state, has become academic. The welfare state is here and will get bigger rather than smaller as the years go by. The only question worth discussing now is what kind of welfare state we want.

The welfare state, of course, must operate on the principle of public funds for public purposes. It is the interpretation of that principle that counts, however. If it is taken to mean that public funds can serve public purposes only when they are spent in and through state-operated institutions, we shall soon have a monistic society. The constantly growing taxes on private income will tend to dry up the sources of funds on which nonstate institutions serving welfare purposes depend (e.g., hospitals, orphanages, homes for the aged, and schools). In short, the groups that want to have and to support such institutions will find that they are competing with their own tax money—and inevitably they will lose.

What is happening to private higher education is a good illustration. In 1950, about 50 percent of American college students attended private colleges and universities. Now fewer than 40 percent do. By 1975, it is predicted, about 25 percent will; by 1985 only 20 percent will.[14] Has this great shift in college attendance from private to state universities taken place because the students or their parents prefer state schools? No, it is because their own taxes have rendered the private colleges noncompetitive.

This kind of result can be avoided not only in education but also in every field of social welfare that government enters, only by a deliberate social determination not to let it happen. The possibility of government doing nothing for social welfare is largely precluded by the needs of modern society. Such a determination can be put into effect, therefore, only by interpreting the principle, "public funds for public purposes," to mean that government can, should, and will aid nongovernmental institutions of social welfare insofar as they perform a public function.

This is the only course open today to a society that wishes to maintain pluralistic institutions to satisfy its welfare needs. The alternative is monism—i.e., that all, or almost all, of our social-welfare institutions will be state-operated and therefore secular. That this alternative is chosen in the name of a particular interpretation of separation of church and state will not make it any the less monistic.

This is the ultimate implication of the Supreme Court's School Prayer and Bible Reading decisions. It is not a theological implication. But one hopes that it is obvious that it is of vast social importance.

Notes

1. *Engel v. Vitale*, 370 U.S. 421 (1962).
2. *School District v. Schempp*, 374 U.S. 203 (1963).
3. 333 U.S. 203 (1948).
4. Ibid., 235.
5. 370 U.S. 421 (1962).
6. 374 U.S. 203 (1963).
7. H.R.J. Res. 9, 88th Cong., 2nd Sess. (1963).
8. "How Moral is Secular Education?" *Christian Century* 73 (1956): 1325.
9. 330 U.S. 1 (1947).
10. Ibid., 23, cited in *Schempp*, 374 U.S. at 218.
11. *Education Between Two Worlds* (New York: Harper & Bros., 1942), 5.
12. *Torcaso v. Watkins*, 367 U.S. 488, 495 (1961).
13. 374 U.S. at 222.
14. Hechinger, "More Than One-Fourth of Nation Attend Schools and Colleges," *New York Times*, September 6, 1964, sect. 4 (Education), 9, col. 1.

4

The Impact of Recent Supreme Court Decisions on Religion in the United States

Bill Klem was once umpiring behind the plate in a National League baseball game. A pitch came in; the batter let it go by, then turned around quickly and said: "That was a ball." Replied Mr. Klem: "It ain't nothing till I call it."

It would probably be too much to say that the religion clauses of the First Amendment "ain't nothing" until the United States Supreme Court "calls" them. Yet they are to a large extent a form to which the Court supplies the content, a skeleton on which the Court puts the flesh and blood. The Court has added most of the flesh and blood only since it decided in the 1940s that the free exercise of religion and the establishment of religion clauses apply to the states as well as to the federal government.[1] American constitutional law on the relations between government and religion is largely a creature of the Court's fashioning in the last one-third of a century.

The purpose of this paper is not to undertake a thorough review and analysis of the Court's jurisprudence on this subject, but only to summarize it briefly in order to assess its impact on religion in the United States. For reasons that will presently appear, some opinions of the Court other than those interpreting the religion clauses will be cited.

The products of the Court's activity that appear to have the most significance for religion in America are the following. The Court has all but closed the door to substantial public aid to church-related schools at

Journal of Church and State (1974)

the elementary and secondary levels. At the same time it has insisted on the secularization of the public schools. The Court has also moved toward identifying religion, in the eyes of the law, with the content of the individual conscience, whatever the content may be. In addition, the Court has surrounded the individual, in several important areas of conduct, with a "right to privacy" that may be limited only by legislation that is justified by a "compelling state interest." The net result is an increasing segregation of religion from the nation's public life. In order to support these conclusions, we now need to review in more detail the Court's recent decisions.

By far the greater number of church-related elementary and secondary schools are Roman Catholic. To consider the question of public financial aid to them, one needs not go farther back than the second school prayer case, *Abington School District v. Schempp* in 1963.[2] The case concerned Bible readings and the recitation of the Lord's Prayer as daily opening exercises in public schools and did not involve parochial schools. But the Court's opinion could be, and was, regarded as having a broader significance than its immediate point at issue because of the test of constitutionality that it laid down for legislation contested as violating the establishment of religion clause. Said Justice Tom Clark in the opinion of the Court:

> The test may be stated as follows: what are the purpose and the primary effect of the enactment? If either is the advancement or inhibition of religion then the enactment exceeds the scope of legislative power as circumscribed by the Constitution. That is to say that to withstand the structures of the Establishment Clause there must be a secular legislative purpose and a primary effect that neither advances nor inhibits religion.[3]

It could be argued that, since parochial and other church-related schools that gave a general elementary or secondary education met the state's secular educational requirements, they served a secular as well as a religious educational purpose. The state, therefore, at either the state or federal level, could aid them by legislation appropriately designed so that the purpose intended and the primary effect achieved was the furtherance of the pupil's secular education. The aid to religious instruction that would result would be real but would be incidental and not constitutionally invalidating. The Court, in fact, accepted and applied this argument in *Board of Education v. Allen* in 1968.[4]

This case concerned a New York state law that required local public school authorities to lend public school textbooks free of charge to all students in grades seven through twelve, including those in private schools. It was argued that, insofar as the textbooks were lent to students in parochial schools, they gave unconstitutional support to religious institutions. Justice Byron White answered for the majority that the Court had long recognized "that religious schools pursue two goals, religious instruction and secular education."[5] The textbooks, designated by public school authorities, would serve the latter and secular purpose which the state might constitutionally further. The provision of free textbooks might perhaps make it more likely that some children would choose to attend a sectarian school. But that was not the state's purpose in providing them, nor could the Court agree that secular textbooks were "in fact instrumental in the teaching of religion."[6] The legislation therefore met the test and was constitutionally valid.[7]

If the state may provide the textbooks for the secular education in religious schools, why may it not subsidize that secular education as a whole? The Court faced and answered that question in 1971, but in the meantime it had decided another case that foreshadowed the answer it would give. In the 1970 case of *Walz v. Tax Commission of the City of New York*[8] the Court upheld the constitutionality of the traditional exemption of religious property from taxation. But in writing the opinion of the Court, Chief Justice Warren Burger defined the purpose of the First Amendment's religion clauses in a way that added a new norm to the test of constitutionality laid down in *Abington v. Schempp*.

"The basic purpose of these provisions," he said, ". . . is to insure that no religion be sponsored or favored, none commanded, and none inhibited." Government is thus committed to a policy of "benevolent neutrality," adherence to which "has prevented the kind of involvement that would tip the balance toward government control of churches or governmental restraint on religious practice." "No perfect or absolute separation [of government and religion] is really possible," he admitted, but the aim of the religion clauses is "to make boundaries to avoid excessive entanglement."[9]

"Excessive entanglement" thus became a third norm, in addition to secular purpose and primary effect, for judging the constitutionality of legislation under the religion clauses. By this norm, direct and substantial aid to parochial schools was struck down in *Lemon v. Kurtzman* and its associated cases in 1971.[10] At issue in these cases were statutes of Rhode Island and Pennsylvania that in varying ways subsidized the teaching of secular subjects in church-related schools by paying a substantial part of the teachers' salaries and, in Pennsylvania, paying also for textbooks and instructional materials.

Chief Justice Burger again wrote the opinion of the Court. The legislative intent of Pennsylvania and Rhode Island, he found, was not to "advance religion." On the contrary, he said, "They have . . . sought to create statutory restrictions designed to guarantee the separation between secular and religious educational functions and to ensure that State financial aid support only the former."[11] But there was the rub. The very effort to make sure that the state-subsidized teacher taught only her secular subject required a "comprehensive, discriminating, and continuing state surveillance . . . to ensure that these restraints are obeyed,"[12] and this created an excessive entanglement between government and religion. The same argument told against the state's power, under the Pennsylvania program, "to inspect and evaluate a church-related school's financial records and to determine which expenditures are religious and which are secular."[13]

On the same day, in *Tilton v. Richardson*,[14] the Court upheld the constitutionality of the Federal Higher Education Facilities Act of 1963, under which construction grants had been received by four Catholic colleges and universities in Connecticut. But pre-college church-related schools were cut off from all but fringe public benefits by a scissors. One blade meant that if they got substantial direct aid without close state surveillance, an "establishment of religion" resulted. The other blade meant that if they got the aid with close state surveillance, "excessive entanglement" resulted.

A way out between the blades might seem to be offered if the state did not subsidize the schools themselves, but reimbursed parents for tuition paid to nonprofit, nonpublic schools. But when New York and Pennsylvania enacted tuition-grant programs, the Court on 25 June 1973 found them to be in violation of the establishment clause,[15] on the ground that such programs, when applied to church-affiliated schools, had "the direct and immediate effect of advancing religion."[16] It is now apparent that parochial schools will be permitted no more than minimal benefits from government. Since parochial schools are closing at the rate of one a day under the pressure of rising costs, the impact of the Court's decisions on them is also predictable. They will cease to be a standard feature of American Catholic life, and moves toward increasing the number of similar schools among such groups as the Orthodox Jews, Episcopalians, and Christian Reformed will be severely inhibited. Justice William Brennan remarked in his concurring opinion in *Lemon v. Kurtzman*, "This Nation long ago committed itself to primary reliance upon publicly supported public education to serve its important goals in secular education."[17] He might have added that under that day's decision the nation was now committed to almost exclusive reliance on public schools.

In the meantime the Court had worked out a doctrine of religious neutrality for the state. In its application to the public schools the doctrine has immediately affected practices that, in the view of the present writer, do not seem to be of great importance in themselves, namely, brief prayers and brief Bible readings as daily opening exercises in the schools. But the concept of neutrality in the light of which the Court has made these applications is broad and far-reaching in its effects.

In *Everson v. Board of Education of Ewing Township*, while upholding the constitutionality of state payment of bus fares for children going to parochial schools, the Court had remarked that the First Amendment "requires the state to be a neutral in its relations with groups of religious believers and non-believers." State power was not to be used to "handicap" religions; neither could it be used to "favor" them.[18] The Court made this doctrine even more explicit in *Torcaso v. Watkins* in 1961, where it repeated that neither a state nor the federal government "can constitutionally pass laws nor impose requirements which aid all religions as against non-believers," and then added, "and neither can aid those religions based on a belief in the existence of God as against those religions founded on different beliefs." In a footnote it listed "Buddhism, Taoism, Ethical Culture and Secular Humanism and others" as example of the latter kind of religion.[19]

It was not surprising, then, when in 1962 in *Engel v. Vitale*[20] the Court found a public school prayer unconstitutional. The prayer had been composed by a group of Jews and Christians in New York in studiously nondenominational terms: "Almighty God, we acknowledge our dependence on Thee, and we beg Thy blessings upon us, our parents, our teachers, and our country." The New York State Board of Regents approved this prayer as suitable for recitation in public schools, but the U.S. Supreme Court found it unconstitutional under the establishment clause.

The essence of the Court's position was that any official public profession of belief in God is an establishment of religion. The prayer, said Justice Hugo Black for the Court, "is a solemn avowal of divine faith and supplication for the blessings of the Almighty,"[21] and as such it "establishes the religious beliefs embodied in" it.[22] It did not matter that the prayer was "nondenominational" or that pupils were free not to join in reciting it, because the "Establishment Clause, unlike the Free Exercise Clause, does not depend upon any showing of direct governmental compulsion and is violated by the enactment of laws which establish an official religion whether those laws operate directly to coerce nonobserving individuals or not.''[23]

It was even less surprising when the following year in *Abington v. Schempp* the Court declared recitation of the Lord's Prayer and Bible reading in public schools unconstitutional. The exercises in question, as the trial court had found, were of a religious character. "Given that finding," said Justice Clark in the majority opinion, "the exercises and the law requiring them are in violation of the Establishment Clause."[24]

Finally, in his concurring opinion in *Lemon v. Kurtzman*, Justice Brennan defined the state's interest in secular education as ''an interest in ensuring that all children within its boundaries acquire a minimum level of competency in certain skills, such as reading, writing, and arithmetic, as well as a minimum amount of information and knowledge in certain subjects such as history, geography, science, literature and law.'' These skills and knowledge could be learned in sectarian as well as public schools, he admitted, though that did not justify subsidizing the sectarian schools.[25] But he did not ask (1) whether the disjunction of this secular education in public schools from all religious beliefs, defined as the Court now defines them, is possible; or (2) whether secular education, defined as he defines it, can be the substance of an adequate education even for young children; or (3) whether his definition of secular education is an accurate description of what actually takes place in public schools. We are apparently to assume, for example, that sex education in public schools imparts "a minimum amount of information and knowledge" utterly unrelated to any scheme of beliefs and values to which the Court would give the status of "religion."

No justice of the Supreme Court has alluded to these questions in any other than the kind of oblique and passing remarks quoted above. A serious discussion of them would seem to be essential to the Court's thesis that government must be completely neutral between religious belief and unbelief, yet is competent to give an education. But the Court does not engage in such discussion. It simply assumes that secular education is neutral education.

The public school, therefore, having been "neutral on the side of God," is now commanded to be neutral between God and whatever His opposite may be. The impact of this conclusion, one might judge, would be heaviest on the Protestant population of the United States. The Catholics never believed very fervently in the nonsectarian, but not really secular, public school of the nineteenth and early twentieth centuries, and the Jews were more interested in getting Christianity out of it than in keeping nondenominational religion in it. But the public school was the "common school" of a Protestant culture, and its complete secularization would appear to signal the passing of that culture.

Yet it cannot be said that the school prayer decisions, now fully ten years old, evoked a strong, still less an effective, protest from American Protestantism. The secularization of public education seems to have been accepted by and large in principle, whatever deviations from it may still persist in local practice. This fact, coupled with the at least partial disappearance of parochial schools, probably means that an increasingly secular culture will have a correspondingly secularized educational system.[26]

The Court's insistence on governmental religious neutrality is also manifested in the tendency it has sometimes shown to take all ultimate beliefs, of whatever nature, as religious beliefs that are equal before the law. Thus it is the position of the belief in the individual's conscience, not the substance of that which is believed, that makes a belief religious for legal purposes. Government must accept as religious beliefs whatever an individual holds as his deepest convictions, even though he himself may deny that they are religious beliefs in the ordinary sense of the term. The result is to formalize and individualize the definition of religion used by the Court. The definition is purely formal inasmuch as it requires only that a belief be ultimate; it is individualized inasmuch as its content is supplied by the individual alone.

The tendency to view religion in this way appeared most clearly in certain conscientious objector cases arising under section 6 (j) of the Universal Military Training and Service Act. This section grants exemption from combatant training and service in the armed forces to those persons who by reason of their religious training and belief are conscientiously opposed to participation in war in any form. The section then defines religious belief as "an individual's belief in a relation to a Supreme Being involving duties superior to those arising from any human relation," but excludes "essentially political, sociological, or philosophical views or a merely personal moral code" as grounds for exemption.

Several applicants for exemption from military service attacked this clause because it did not exempt nonreligious conscientious objectors and discriminated among different forms of religious expression, thereby allegedly violating the religion clauses of the First Amendment and the due process clause of the Fifth Amendment. The Court dealt with this complaint in 1965 in *U. S. v. Seeger* and its associated cases.[27]

In an opinion delivered by Justice Clark, the Court noted that none of the applicants for exemption claimed to be an atheist or attacked the statute on that ground. The question, therefore, was not "one between theistic and atheistic beliefs."[28] All of the applicants sought exemption with the terms of the act, i.e., on the basis of "religious belief." But theirs were highly individual beliefs in some kind of ultimate reality, and one of them, Seeger, in his own words combined "skepticism or disbelief in the existence of God" with "a religious faith in a purely ethical creed."[29]

The Court judged these beliefs sufficient to qualify applicants for exemption from military service. The act, it said, must be understood to encompass

> all sincere religious beliefs which are based upon a power or being, or upon a faith, to which all else is subordinate or upon which all else is ultimately dependent. The test might be stated in these words: A sincere and meaningful belief which occupies in the life of its possessor a place parallel to that fulfilled by the God of those admittedly qualifying for the exemption comes within the statutory definition.[30]

There may seem to be an objective element remaining in the above definition of religious belief, namely, that it must at least have as its object "a power or being . . . to which all else is subordinate or upon which all else is ultimately dependent." But the Court dispelled this impression as illusory in a subsequent case in 1970, in which it became clear that its definition of religion was cast in purely subjective terms.

There was no majority opinion in this case, *Welsh v. U.S.*,[31] but Justice Black announced the judgment of the Court and wrote a plurality opinion in which Justices Brennan, William Douglas, and Thurgood Marshall joined him; and on the point relevant to this paper Justice John Marshall Harlan concurred in a separate opinion. Justice Black explained that in order to avoid "a preference to those who believed in a conventional God as opposed to those who did not," the Court in *U.S. v. Seeger* had extended the meaning of religious belief "so as to embrace *all* religions."[32] The Court was then faced with the problem of deciding which beliefs were "religious" within the meaning of sect. 6 (j) of the Universal Military Training and Service Act.

Justice Black stated the Court's answer to this problem in the following terms. "What is necessary under *Seeger* for a registrant's conscientious objection to all war to be 'religious' within the meaning of sect. 6 (j) is that this opposition to war stem from the registrant's moral, ethical, or religious beliefs about what is right and wrong and that these beliefs be held with the strength of traditional religious convictions."

It follows that "beliefs that are purely ethical or moral in source and content" are sufficient as a basis for exemption if held with the requisite strength.[33] It did not matter, therefore, that Welsh explicitly denied that his beliefs were religious. He held them deeply and as a matter of principle, not on "considerations of policy, pragmatism, or expediency." That was enough to make them religious beliefs within the meaning of the statute and to qualify him for exemption from military service.[34]

It might be argued that the Court's interpretation of "religion" and "religious belief" in the *Seeger* and *Welsh* cases should not be taken too seriously, since the Court was obviously engaged in a tortured interpretation of the terms in order to extend their coverage to those philosophical and moral views that the act intended not to recognize as grounds for exemption. Justice Harlan made this objection in his concurring opinion. He concurred with the judgment of the Court nonetheless, because he agreed that under the establishment clause those views could not be excluded from coverage. It might be judicial legerdemain to call them religious beliefs, but if the act were interpreted as favoring properly religious beliefs, it would be an unconstitutional establishment of religion. Therefore, he concluded, "If the exemption is to be given application, it must encompass the class of individuals it purports to exclude, those whose beliefs emanate from a purely moral, ethical, or philosophical source. The common denominator must be the intensity of moral conviction with which a belief is held."[35]

It would seem, then, that on the essential point, Justice Harlan and the four Justices who joined in the plurality opinion were in agreement. Whether or not certain convictions are properly described as religious beliefs, the law must recognize them as having equal standing with those beliefs generally recognized as religious and may consider only the common feature shared by both classes of belief, that is, the intensity of moral conviction with which they are held. To favor some beliefs over others because of their objective content, e.g., personal responsibility to God, would be to establish religion. The only characteristic of a belief of which the law may take account is the purely subjective one of the strength of conviction with which the subject holds it.

Seeger and *Welsh* were cases arising under the establishment clause, and the subjective definition of religion that the Court employed in them would cause obvious difficulties if applied in cases arising under the free exercise clause. The Court in fact backed off in 1972 from its earlier definition in order to decide a free exercise case.

This case, *Wisconsin v. Yoder*,[36] involved members of the Amish religion who were convicted of violating Wisconsin's compulsory school attendance law because they refused to send their children to school after the eighth grade. The defendants pleaded that their religion forbade further formal schooling for their children and that by enforcing the school attendance law on them, Wisconsin was depriving them of their right to the free exercise of their religion.

The Court acknowledged that the state had a valid interest in promoting universal education to age sixteen but made the case turn on the issue of whether it was ''a state interest of sufficient magnitude to override the interest claiming protection under the Free Exercise Clause.''[37] For reasons which need not be detailed here, the Court decided that Wisconsin's interest was not great enough and that an exception to the law must be made for the Amish.

The Court was careful to make it plain, however, that the interest protected by the free exercise clause in this case was rooted in the beliefs of the Amish not only as held in their minds but also as embodied in their whole way of life, and that these beliefs were religious. As Chief Justice Burger put it in the opinion of the Court,

A way of life, however virtuous and admirable, may not be interposed as a barrier to reasonable state regulation of education if it is based on purely secular considerations; to have the protection of the Religion Clauses, the claims must be rooted in religious belief. Although a determination of what is a ''religious'' belief or practice entitled to constitutional protection may present a most delicate question,[38] the very concept of ordered liberty precludes allowing every person to make his own standards on matters of conduct in which society as a whole has important interests. Thus, if the Amish asserted their claims because of their subjective evaluation and rejection of the contemporary secular values accepted by the majority, much as Thoreau rejected the social values of his time and isolated himself at Walden Pond, their claim would not rest on a religious basis. Thoreau's choice was philosophical and personal rather than religious, and such belief does not rise to the demands of the Religion Clauses.[39]

But the beliefs of the Amish did rise to the required level because ''the traditional way of life of the Amish is not merely a matter of personal preference, but one of deep religious conviction, shared by an organized group, and intimately related to daily living.''[40]

The contrast with the *Seeger* and *Welsh* cases is clear. So, for that matter, is the contrast with *Torcaso v. Watkins*. In the above cases, the Court held that to favor belief in God over other beliefs would be an establishment of religion. To avoid such an establishment, religion should be given a subjective definition that would cover all ultimate beliefs of whatever nature and would treat them all equally. In the *Yoder* case, however, the Court granted an exception to the Wisconsin school attendance law but insisted that only a clearly religious group whose exercise of religion clearly required the exception could take advantage of it.

Chief Justice Burger adverted to this apparent contradiction when he said in his *Yoder* opinion: "The Court must not ignore the danger that an exception from a general obligation of citizenship on religious grounds may run afoul of the Establishment Clause, but that danger cannot be allowed to prevent any exception no matter how vital it may be to the protection of values promoted by the right of free exercise." The contradiction could be resolved in practice, he felt, by "preserving doctrinal flexibility and recognizing the need for a sensible and realistic application of the Religion Clauses."[41]

The sensible and realistic application seems to mean that the establishment clause must be construed as broadly as possible in order to avoid governmental favor to traditional theistic beliefs. This line of thought, pursued to the end, leads to a purely subjective definition of religion. But where the free exercise clause appears to demand an exception from a general legal obligation for an atypical group such as the Amish, religion must be defined more strictly and objectively in order to narrow the exception.

To complete the picture, where it is judged desirable to uphold a law, such as a Sunday closing law, that in fact favors the religious practices of the major religious groups, the law will be interpreted as merely secular in its purposes in order to save it from attack under the establishment clause.[42] When Sabbatarians claim an exemption from compliance with a Sunday closing law under the free exercise clause, their claim may be denied on the ground that the law is secular in its aims and does not prevent them from exercising their religion, though it may indirectly burden that exercise.[43]

The premise that unifies these positions was stated by Chief Justice Burger in *Lemon v. Kurtzman* in these words: "The Constitution decrees that religion must be a private matter for the individual, the family, and the institutions of private choice."[44] Government, being public, must be neutral toward all shades of religious belief and unbelief and must pursue purely secular goals by purely secular means. But the secular aims that government pursues will be limited by private rights, among them the free exercise of religion, that can be restricted or overridden only upon a showing of a "compelling state interest."

The doctrine that balances private rights against ''compelling state interest'' extends far beyond the scope of the religion clauses. It appeared in its first application to a freedom of religion case, however, in *Sherbert v. Verner* in 1963.[45] Verner, a Seventh-Day Adventist, was denied unemployment compensation benefits in South Carolina because she would not accept employment that involved working on Saturday in violation of the tenets of her faith. In an opinion by Justice Brennan, the Supreme Court held that by forcing her to a choice between working on Saturday and doing without unemployment compensation, South Carolina deprived her of the free exercise of her religion.

The disqualification for benefits clearly imposed a burden on Verner's practice of her religion, the Court found. The question then became whether this incidental burden ''may be justified by a 'compelling state interest in the regulation of a subject within the State's constitutional power to regulate.' ''[46] The Court found no such state interest demonstrated by South Carolina and, in an illuminating passage, contrasted its holding in this case with its decision of *Braunfeld v. Brown*, a Sunday closing law case:

> The Court recognized that the Sunday closing law which that decision sustained undoubtedly served ''to make the practice of [the Orthodox Jewish merchants'] . . . religious beliefs more expensive,'' 336 U.S., at 605. But the statute was nevertheless saved by a countervailing factor which finds no equivalent in the instant case—a strong state interest in providing one uniform day of rest for all workers. That secular objective could be achieved, the Court found, only by declaring Sunday to be that day of rest. Requiring exemptions for Sabbatarians, while theoretically possible, appeared to present an administrative problem of magnitude, or to afford the exempted class so great a competitive advantage that such a requirement would have rendered the entire statutory scheme unworkable. In the present case no such justifications underlie the determination of the state court that appellant's religion makes her ineligible to receive benefits.[47]

The above test, by which a compelling state interest is weighed against the free exercise of religion, can be and has been used in cases involving rights other than those of free exercise. A significant line of such cases began in 1965 with *Griswold v. Connecticut*,[48] in which the Court recognized or created a constitutional ''right of privacy.'' Justice Douglas, who wrote the opinion of the Court, admitted that this right was not mentioned in the Constitution. But, he argued, ''specific guarantees in the Bill of Rights have penumbras, formed by emanations from those guarantees that help give them life and substance. Various guarantees create zones of privacy.''[49]

At issue in this case was a Connecticut law specifically forbidding the use of contraceptives and a general law forbidding anyone to aid or counsel another person to commit a crime. The appellants in the case were the executive director of the Connecticut Planned Parenthood League and a physician who, in the words of Justice Douglas, "gave information, instruction, and medical advice to *married persons* as to the means of preventing conception.''[50] It was important in the view of Justice Douglas that the recipients of the information were married persons, because he concluded:

> The present case . . . concerns a relationship lying within the zone of privacy created by several fundamental constitutional guarantees. And it concerns a law which, in forbidding the *use* of contraceptives rather than regulating their manufacture or sale, seeks to achieve its goals by means having a maximum destructive impact upon that relationship. Such a law cannot stand in light of the familiar principle, so often applied by this Court, that a "governmental purpose to control or prevent activities constitutionally subject to state regulation may not be achieved by means which sweep unnecessarily broadly and thereby invade the area of protected freedom." *NAACP v. Alabama*, 377 U.S. 288, 307. Would we allow the police to search the sacred precincts of marital bedrooms for telltale signs of the use of contraceptives? The very idea is repulsive to the notions of privacy surrounding the marriage relationship.[51]

But it eventually became apparent to the Court that the right of privacy established in the *Griswold* case could not be confined within the bond of marriage. Justice Brennan explained in 1972 in *Eisenstadt v. Baird*:

> If under Griswold the distribution of contraceptives to married persons cannot be prohibited, a ban on distribution to unmarried persons would be equally impermissible. It is true that in Griswold the right of privacy in question inhered in the marital relationship. Yet the marital couple is not an independent entity with a mind and heart of its own, but an association of two individuals each with a separate intellectual and emotional makeup. If the right of privacy means anything, it is the right of the *individual*, married or single, to be free from unwarranted governmental intrusion into matters so fundamentally affecting a person as the decision whether to bear or beget a child.[52]

The process of balancing the ''right of privacy'' against a ''compelling state interest'' finally came to term (if the phrase may be permitted) in 1973 when the Court explicitly used these concepts to find state laws prohibiting abortion unconstitutional. In the Court's opinion in *Roe v. Wade*,[53] Justice Harry Blackmun argued, first, that "a right of personal privacy . . . does exist under the Constitution" and includes "personal rights that can be deemed 'fundamental' or 'implicit in the concept of ordered liberty.' "[54] Second, he said, "Where certain 'fundamental rights' are involved, the Court has held that regulation limiting these rights may be justified only by a 'compelling state interest.' "[55]

Justice Blackmun went on to conclude that "the right of personal privacy includes the abortion decision, but . . . this right is not unqualified and must be considered against important state interest in regulation."[56] "Logically, of course," he admitted, "a legitimate state interest in this area need not stand or fall on acceptance of the belief that life begins at conception or at some other point prior to live birth."[57] But the Court, he said, "need not resolve the difficult question of when life begins."[58] It was sufficient to note that it was a question disputed among experts and to conclude that the state might not "by adopting one theory of life, . . . override the rights of the pregnant woman that are at stake."[59] At this point consideration of the rights of the unborn child and of the state's interest in protecting it ceased. All that remained to be considered was "the State's important and legitimate interest in the health of the mother," in respect to which "the 'compelling' point, in the light of present medical knowledge, is at approximately the end of the first trimester." After that point "a State may regulate the abortion procedure to the extent that the regulation reasonably relates to the preservation and protection of maternal health."[60]

The last three cases discussed here did not arise under the religion clauses. But they are worth mentioning because they reveal a development in the Court's jurisprudence that will have a significant impact on religion in the United States. The Court is no longer concerned only with the free exercise of religion or the other rights specifically named in the First Amendment. It now takes and decides cases involving a general "right of privacy" that can be limited only by a "compelling state interest," and the Court is the sole judge of both of these.

The Court may be moving itself into a position similar to the one it staked out for itself during the forty years in which it balanced "freedom of contract" against the state's interest in protecting public health and safety, and usually found the latter wanting. The Court will then be the supreme arbiter of the American conscience. The conscience it will both reflect and shape is likely to be a secular and highly individualistic one.

The bias of the Court's recent decisions is toward broadening the freedom of the individual and removing large areas of moral choice from public control. The Court's actions may only reflect the disintegration of the moral consensus, rooted in a common religious tradition, that underlays laws on such matters as contraception and abortion. But since the Court is not itself a legislative body, it cannot repeal laws it deems no longer supported by public opinion. It has to declare that it is beyond the power of any legislature to make such laws at all in the absence of a compelling state interest. This implies that, even if there were a moral consensus behind a particular law, it would still be unconstitutional as a violation of the right of privacy. Certainly plaintiffs will not be lacking to urge that argument against an ever wider range of laws regulating personal conduct. Suits contesting laws against homosexual acts and laws prohibiting euthanasia, for example, must now be anticipated.

One may cheer these plaintiffs on as champions of liberty or decry them as agents of society's moral decay. But, however one looks at the matter, the decision on the right of privacy that the Court has made and those it may make in the future tend to erode the police power of the state to protect public morals and to narrow the area in which the community's conscience may express itself in law. Insofar as the conscience is formed by religious belief, the impact of the Court's decisions will again be to limit the influence of religion on public policy and to segregate it in the area occupied by ''the individual, the family, and the institutions of private choice.''

Whether the religious conscience will be allowed to prevail even in the institutions of private choice is not altogether clear. Private hospitals, for instance, may be faced with court orders commanding them to allow abortions to be performed in their facilities, either because they receive public financial aid or because they are the only hospitals serving the public in their area. The *New York Times* reported on 2 July 1973 that the American Civil Liberties Union and the National Association to Repeal Abortion Laws have begun a nationwide campaign to obtain such court orders. But no case raising this issue has yet come to the U.S. Supreme Court.

A distinct issue that may soon come before the Court is whether the right of privacy, being a constitutional right, must be subsidized by the public for those who cannot pay for its exercise from their own resources. The *New York Daily News* reported on 21 February 1973 that the Court had asked the U.S. solicitor general for an opinion on whether it should review the decision of a lower court ordering abortions to be provided at state expense for recipients of Medicaid. If the Court should take the case and affirm the decision of the lower court, it will have committed itself even more strongly to a secular and individualistic ethic.

If it should take this step, the Court will open itself to the kind of criticism recently voiced by Professor Ralph McInerny of the University of Notre Dame:

> What clearly puzzles many religious people is that, having accepted the wisdom of the idea that they have no right to impose their beliefs on others, they are in turn being asked to support laws and policies which enforce practices with which they are in profound disagreement. It is one thing to concede that a judgment about the immorality of contraception does not call for a public policy outlawing the use of contraceptives on the part of those who do not share the moral judgment. It is something else to have one's tax money used to disseminate contraceptive devices to "underdeveloped people" both at home and abroad. So too with abortion, day-care centers, euthanasia, etc. Public policy seems less and less a neutral protection of rights than the active promotion of a view of life incompatible with religious convictions.

McInerny sees this development as producing a profound alienation of religious people—he is obviously thinking principally of Catholics— from the American state. "Faith," he says, "is no longer something which can be identified with the wider community, with America and its institutions. The State is no longer secular or neutral. It has become the enemy."[61]

Some will no doubt consider McInerny's views alarmist or even reactionary. But the point he makes is one that has to be taken into account in an assessment of the impact of the Court's recent decisions on religion in America. The Court has worked out a doctrine of official religious neutrality that may be expressed in the formula: Neutrality = strict secularity of public institutions + little or no public financial aid to religious institutions + lessening of public restrictions on individual moral choice. The formula embodies the assumptions of liberal individualism and conceivably might work well enough in a society dedicated to the principles of laissez faire. But whether these assumptions are realistic when applied in a pluralistic society governed by a welfare state is open to question. It may be that, in its effort to achieve neutrality, the Court has thrown the resources of the state behind the establishment of what it once, perhaps in a moment of rashness, called the religion of secular humanism.

Notes

1. *Cantwell v. Connecticut,* 310 U.S. 296 (1940); *Everson v. Board of Education of Ewing Township,* 330 U.S. 1 (1947).
2. 374 U.S. 203.
3. Ibid., 222.
4. 392 U.S. 236.
5. Ibid., 245.
6. Ibid., 244, 248.
7. On the same day the Court decided *Flast v. Cohen,* 392 U.S. 83, granting federal taxpayers standing to sue in cases arising under the establishment clause. This of course made it easier to contest the constitutionality of federal statutes that benefited church-related schools.
8. 397 U.S. 664.
9. Ibid., 669–70.
10. 403 U.S. 602.
11. Ibid., 613.
12. Ibid., 619.
13. Ibid., 621–22.
14. 403 U.S. 672.
15. *Committee for Public Education & Religious Liberty v. Nyquist* 37 L.Ed. 2nd 948; *Sloan v. Lemon,* ibid., 939.
16. *Committee v. Nyquist,* ibid., 969, n. 39. In this case and the companion case of *Levitt v. Committee,* ibid., 736, the Court also declared unconstitutional the reimbursement of parochial schools for such expenses as maintenance, repairs and record-keeping.
17. 403 U.S. 602, 658.
18. 330 U.S. 1, 18.
19. 367 U.S. 488, 495.
20. 370 U.S. 421
21. Ibid., 424.
22. Ibid., 430.
23. Ibid.
24. 374 U.S. 203, 223.
25. 403 U.S. 602, 655.
26. Under *McCollum v. Board of Education,* 333 U.S. 203 (1948), and *Zorach v. Clauson,* 343 U.S. 306 (1952), "released-time" religious instruction classes are unconstitutional if held inside a public school, but not if held outside it. Opinions vary on the utility of such classes in providing for the religious instruction of the young.
27. 380 U.S. 163.
28. Ibid., 173.
29. Ibid., 166.
30. Ibid., 176.

31. 398 U.S. 333.

32. Ibid., 338.

33. Ibid., 341–43.

34. Ibid., 338.

35. Ibid., 358.

36. 32 L.Ed.2nd 15.

37. Ibid., 358.

38. A footnote at this point refers to *Welsh v. U.S.*, 398 U.S. 333 (1970), and *U.S. v. Ballard* 322 U.S. 78 (1944).

39. *Wisconsin v. Yoder*, supra, 25.

40. Ibid.

41. Ibid., 28.

42. *McGowan v. Maryland*, 366 U.S. 420 (1961).

43. *Braunfeld v. Brown*, 366 U.S. 599 (1961).

44. 403 U.S. 602, 625.

45. 374 U.S. 398.

46. Ibid., 403; The Court was quoting itself in an earlier freedom of assembly case, *NAACP v. Button*, 371 U.S. 415, 438 (1963).

47. Ibid., 408–9.

48. 381 U.S. 479.

49. Ibid., 484.

50. Ibid., 480.

51. Ibid., 485.

52. 31 L.Ed.2nd 349, 362.

53. 35 L.Ed.2nd 147.

54. Ibid., 176. The interior quotations are from *Palko v. Connecticut*, 302 U.S. 319, 325 (1937).

55. Ibid., 178.

56. Ibid., 177–78.

57. Ibid., 175.

58. Ibid., 181.

59. Ibid., 182.

60. Ibid.

61. ''The American Heresy,'' *Worldview*, 15 (May 1972): 46.

5

The Girl in the Glass Box

Imagine, if you will, that you are kidnapped, hustled into a plane, and flown for many hours, in what direction you do not know. In the middle of the night you are equipped with a parachute and shoved out into the dark. You come to earth on a brightly lighted street in a foreign city. The signs you read and the words you hear people speaking are in a language that is completely strange to you. Then your eyes light on a display of pornography. Would you not exclaim: "Thank God, I'm in a liberal democracy!"

Of course you would, for you know, as we all know, that pornography is the hallmark of the modern democratic state, the outward sign by which we distinguish the substance of liberty from tyranny. Liberals will lay their hands upon their hearts and assure you that, while as mature and sophisticated adults they have of course seen *Deep Throat* and read *The Story of O*, they found both these works of art boring and that their firsthand acquaintance with pornography is in fact very limited. Nonetheless, they will fight to the death for the pornographer's right to produce the stuff and the customer's right to buy it, because they know that it is the foundation stone of liberty. If it crumbles, the whole edifice of freedom collapses.

The thinking that leads to this conviction is admirably illustrated by the opinion of the U.S. Supreme Court in the Case of the Girl in the Glass Box,[1] which was decided on June 1, 1981. Justice Byron White wrote the opinion of the Court, and students of his earlier opinions in First Amendment cases may find his views here somewhat surprising. But, although Justice White is a very intelligent man and ordinarily says

The Human Life Review (1983)

intelligent things, he is a judge and as such is bound by precedents. Presumably he felt that the precedents dictated the conclusion at which the Court arrived here. Stare decisis is a sound rule but it does exact a price.

But let us turn to the facts of the case. The glass box was located in an "adult" bookstore in Mount Ephraim, N.J., a small dormitory suburb lying between the cities of Philadelphia, Pa., and Camden, N.J. The bookstore in question sold "adult" books, magazines, and films and also had, in the Court's words, "coin-operated devices by virtue of which a customer could sit in a booth, insert a coin and watch an adult film." At a later date it installed a similar device that allowed the customer, by inserting a coin, to watch a young woman dance in the nude in the glass box. How long he got to watch her is not mentioned in the Court's opinion, but a report in the *New York Times*[2] on the flourishing sex industry in New York City states that in a similar establishment off Times Square, one coin bought "about 60 seconds of viewing." Mount Ephraim may have been more generous than the Big City—small towns usually are—but the viewing time bought by one coin was still doubtless short. Those who wished to view longer could, of course, insert more coins.

The installation of the glass box led to the prosecution of Messrs. Schad et al., owners of the bookstore, and they were fined in the municipal court for violating Mount Ephraim's zoning ordinance, which forbade all live entertainment in the area zoned for commercial use. The state courts upheld their conviction on appeal, and the U.S. Supreme Court then took their case for review. "Their principal claim," as that Court stated in its opinion, "is that the imposition of criminal penalties under an ordinance prohibiting all live entertainment, including nonobscene, nude dancing, violated their rights of free expression guaranteed by the First and Fourteenth Amendments of the United States Constitution."[3] On the issue thus defined, Mount Ephraim lost and its zoning ordinance was declared unconstitutional.

Mount Ephraim evidently had made a rash attempt to prevent the kind of entertainment going on in the glass box by laying down a blanket prohibition of all live entertainment in its commercial zone. Its real and deeper fault, however, was to overlook the essential difference between nonobscene nude dancing and obscene nude dancing. The latter is a distinct legal category. There seem to be no known examples of it, but we may be sure that if the municipal authorities ever should discover a certifiably obscene nude dance being performed in Mount Ephraim, the Supreme Court would agree that it was not protected by the First and Fourteenth Amendments. In the meantime, the Court will regard nude dancing as nonobscene and protected against heavy-handed efforts to ban it.

But, some quibbler will ask, how do we know just what was going on in the glass box? The Court did not address itself to this question (the most interesting facts in this case are the ones that the Court leaves out of its opinion). Since I have not myself made the journey to Mount Ephraim and inserted the requisite coin in the glass box, I cannot pronounce apodictically on what was going on inside it. But it seems a safe assumption that the young woman was not doing solo numbers from *Giselle* or *Swan Lake*. More likely, she was simply gyrating or, when she got tired of standing in one place, prancing about in the nude.

Was this, in any proper sense of the term, dancing? Again, the Court did not say, and it is easy to understand why it did not. After all, a court that cannot decide when human life begins will hardly venture to determine the point at which mere physical motion becomes dancing. The presumption therefore had to be that the girl was dancing.

Since she was dancing, she was engaged in "expression" and "communication." What was she expressing; what message was she trying to communicate? There is no hint in the Court's opinion that anyone thought to ask her (and she might have been astonished if the question had been put to her). I do recall that when the Court of Appeals of the State of New York struck down as unconstitutional a law prohibiting nude and seminude "dancing" in barrooms, a newspaper reporter asked one of the dancers for her opinion. "Listen," she said, "there are a lot of sick guys out there, and it's better they should be in here looking at me than outside molesting women." Your professional nude dancer, untutored in the law though she is, and surely innocent of any knowledge of sociology, sometimes has an earthy realism that would repay study by the members of the Supreme Court. The Justices, however, did not ask what the girl in the glass box was doing or thought she was doing and were content to argue from the Cartesian premise, "I dance, therefore I express myself."

They were thus able to wrap the girl, if we may so phrase it, in the mantle of freedom of expression, which, as everyone knows, is guaranteed by the First Amendment. It is true that the amendment does not use the term "expression." Instead it says: "Congress shall make no law . . . abridging the freedom of speech, or of the press." The amendment, therefore, in its own terms, guarantees the freedom of speech and press, and a careless reader might jump to the conclusion that the framers of the amendment intended the right to utter and to print words. He might also conclude that the use of words is protected only against abridgement by Congress, not by the states or municipalities. But this would only betray the reader's ignorance of constitutional law. This, as fashioned by the Court in a long line of precedents, tells us that "the freedom of speech, or of the press" in the First Amendment really means "freedom of expression," and that, through the Fourteenth Amendment, this freedom is protected equally against infringement by the national, state, or local levels of government.

We thus move through a series of abstractions: nudity, as such, is not obscene; nude dancing is nonetheless dancing; dancing is a form of expression or communication; freedom of expression is the meaning of the freedom of speech or of the press in the First Amendment; and the First Amendment binds every government in the country. As we progress through these abstractions, the concrete reality that is the subject matter of the case drops out, i.e., the girl in the glass box. The Court thus puts itself in the position of the judge who will not allow himself to know what everyone knows. As Chief Justice Warren Burger said in his dissenting opinion, in which Justice William Rehnquist joined him,

> the issue in the case that we have before us is not whether Mount Ephraim may ban traditional live entertainment but whether it may ban nude dancing, which is used as the "bait" to induce customers into the appellant's book store. When, and if, this ordinance is used to prevent a high school performance of "The Sound of Music," for example, the Court can deal with that problem.[4]

The Court's answer to the Chief Justice was that the issue was the constitutional validity of a zoning ordinance that on its face would ban "The Sound of Music" as well as nude dancing because it prohibited all live entertainment. If the ordinance adversely affected a mere property interest, the Court said, it might stand as an exercise of "municipal power to control land use."[5] But this ordinance could not be allowed to stand because it "totally excludes all live entertainment, including nonobscene nude dancing that is otherwise protected by the First Amendment."[6]

But to say this is only once again to subsume the girl in the glass box into an abstraction. The reality with which the case was concerned, as the Court itself described it, was a peep show and nothing but a peep show. In the key move in its opinion, on which all else depended, the

Court chose to turn the peep show into a form of expression protected by the First Amendment and equally entitled to protection with all other forms of expression. On this premise our most fundamental democratic liberties are supposed to stand.

That is why pornography prevails throughout the democratic world. The writ of the U.S. Supreme Court does not run beyond our borders, and one cannot attribute to its decisions the flourishing state of pornography in other countries. But the reasoning is everywhere the same: freedom of expression is a seamless robe, and we cannot pull one thread out of its fabric lest the whole garment should unravel. Expression is expression is expression, and all forms of it stand or fall together. This conviction has little to do with devotion to democracy, for there is no reason to believe that the successful operation of democratic institutions depends on the availability of peep shows. It really rests on the liberal belief that all expressions ultimately express tastes and preferences, all of which are equally entitled to protection because they are all equally subjective.

It would be cynical to see in the liberal view a desire to buy off the masses with a mindless freedom of expression in order to win their submission to the yoke of ever-increasing state regulation of the rest of their lives. It is kinder and probably more just to assume that liberals really believe what they say. The question is whether the rest of us should believe it.

Notes

1. *Schad et al. v. Borough of Mount Ephraim*, 452 U.S. 61 (1981).
2. February 10, 1981, B6.
3. *Schad v. Mt. Ephraim*, 65.
4. Ibid., 86.
5. Ibid., 68.
6. Ibid., 76.

6

Natural Law and Judicial Review

Natural law, at least as a theory of natural rights, is not foreign to the American tradition. We began our career as an independent nation with an appeal to nature and nature's God, who had endowed men at the creation with certain inalienable rights. Nor is natural law foreign to our Constitution and our laws. American law incorporates many principles of natural justice, or of what the legislators believed were such, and so does the Constitution. Few, for instance, will doubt that the framers of the Thirteenth Amendment banned slavery because they thought that it violated the natural right of the slaves and was morally wrong.

But whether the American practice of judicial review authorizes judges to appeal directly to natural law, or to read into the Constitution natural (or ''human'') rights not mentioned in that document is another and much controverted question. It is the one, and the only one, that I mean to discuss here.

Judicial review as understood and practiced in this country is the power of courts to declare acts of legislatures or executive organs of government null and void because they conflict with the constitution, whether it be the constitution of the nation or of a state. The question to which I shall address myself here is not whether there is a natural law binding on all human beings, or whether it binds legislatures and executives in conscience. It will be simply whether judges are empowered to enforce natural law in performing their function of judicial review.

It is not necessary here to scan all the theories of natural law that there are and to decide which is the correct one. For the present purpose it will be enough to call natural law any binding moral principles not

Public Affairs Quarterly (1993)

made by men but derived by reason from the nature of things or, more usually, from the nature of man. Since, as human beings we are endowed with free wills, natural law for us is moral law, since we can act against it, but are obliged to choose to act in accordance with it, because to violate it would be violating our own nature. If we acknowledge God as the Creator and Author of nature, to violate our nature is also to disobey God.

Natural law, in any conception of it, is recognized by reason as superior to human will and binding upon it. To come to the point of this essay, it is quite possible to accept natural law and still doubt the authority of judges to enforce it directly and not through the medium of positive, man-made law.

That was the position, for example, that Edmund Burke took. Burke, of course, was a member of the British Parliament, which did not and does not recognize the power of judicial review. Furthermore, the passages I shall cite below were written in the 1770s, before there was an American Constitution, and so were written in ignorance of what our Constitution would contain. Nonetheless, what Burke said about the power of judges strikes me as correct and fully applicable to our practice of judicial review.

Burke certainly believed in natural law and often appealed to it. It was this law that he had in mind when he wrote to the Sheriffs of Bristol (whose member of Parliament he then was): "Legislators ought to do what lawyers cannot; for they have no other rules to bind them, but the great principles of reason and equity, and the general sense of mankind."[1] Not so, however, with judges:

> A Judge, a person exercising a Judicial Capacity—is neither to apply to original Justice alone; nor to a discretionary application of it. He goes to Justice and discretion only second hand, and through the medium of some superiours. He is to work neither upon his opinion of the one nor of the other. But upon a fixed Rule, of which he has not the making, but singly and solely the application to the Case. The very Idea of Law is to exclude discretion in the Judge.[2]

Burke's view of the function of a judge is what I understand Judge Robert Bork's to be. I have heard Bork described as a positivist; since I have not read everything he has written, I cannot say for sure that he has never taken a positivist position. I can say that I am not convinced by the quotations from his works that I have seen alleged to show that he is a legal positivist, i.e., one who holds that positive law is the only law, on the ground that law is only what is enacted by a competent human authority, and is nothing else. All that Bork seems to be saying is what I read in his book, *The Tempting of America:* "I am far from denying that there is a natural law, but I do deny both that we have given judges the authority to enforce it, and that judges have any greater access to that law than do the rest of us."[3] Bork's words are fully compatible both with a belief in natural law and with the American principle of judicial review. That principle means only that courts are empowered to judge the constitutionality of the acts of the other branches of government, which is to say that when one of those acts conflicts with the written Constitution, a court is obliged to uphold the Constitution in preference to the legislative or executive act. It does not imply either the right or the obligation of judges to appeal to natural law against positive law.

Nor does it imply that governments are not bound by natural law. Joseph Grano, a professor of law at Wayne State University and one of Bork's few academic defenders, explains: "The issue that Bork's academic critics obfuscated is not the substantive one of whether government should behave morally, but rather the procedural one of *who should decide* in a democratic society what morality requires."[4] Fervent believers in natural law sometimes seem to overlook the fact that natural law is not self-applying. Some human agency must recognize it and apply it to action. In a modern society, if the action is to be performed or regulated by an organ of government, some human entity with the power to make law must translate the principle of natural law into positive law. Bork's answer, to which I myself subscribe, is that under the American Constitution that agency is not the courts of law, not even the U.S. Supreme Court.

Judicial review got into our national Constitution in order to solve a major problem that confronted the Constitutional Convention of 1787: how to keep the states properly subordinate to the Constitution and to national laws, as they had not been kept under the Articles of Confederation. The original proposal set before the Convention was to give Congress a veto over all state legislation that it deemed unconstitutional. But the Convention was unable to agree on whether there should be such a congressional veto or, if so, what the extent of the veto power should be: James Madison, the Father of the Constitution, wanted it to be unlimited.

On July 17, when the congressional veto was definitively rejected, Luther Martin of Maryland proposed to vest the power to negate state laws in the courts. His proposal was unanimously accepted, and became the supremacy clause in Article VI of the Constitution as we now have it: "This Constitution, and the Laws of the United States which shall be made in Pursuance thereof; and all Treaties made, or which shall be made, under the Authority of the United States, shall be the supreme Law of the Land, and the Judges in every State shall be bound thereby, any Thing in the Constitution or Laws of any State to the Contrary notwithstanding."

The supremacy clause is a positive law in a constitution that is itself a positive law, framed by the Constitutional Convention but enacted by the sovereign people in the ratifying conventions that met in each state. To say this is simply to recognize a fact, that the Constitution is the highest positive law in this country. It does not imply that the will of the people is not subordinate to natural law, or that anything is moral simply because they enact it. The supremacy clause, however, obliges the judges in every state to uphold the national Constitution, laws, and treaties in preference to the constitution and laws of their own state. Their power to do so derives from and is implicit in their obligation.

The supremacy clause, on its face, binds only state judges. Chief Justice John Marshall of the U.S. Supreme Court, however, in the famous case of *Marbury v. Madison* in 1803, found the power of the Court to declare acts of Congress unconstitutional to be implicit in the nature of a written constitution:

> The constitution is either a superior paramount law, unchangeable by ordinary means, or it is on a level with ordinary legislative acts, and, like other acts, is alterable when the legislature shall please to alter it. If the former part of the alternative is true, then a legislative act, contrary to the constitution is not law: if the latter part be true, then written constitutions are absurd attempts, on the part of the people, to limit a power, in its own nature, illimitable.[5]

I am personally satisfied that Marshall's argument is a sound one. But notice that it rests entirely on the premise that the Constitution is a positive law, differing from ordinary statutes only in being the highest positive law, because it was made by the ultimate sovereign, the people. The power granted to judges by the Constitution is the power to uphold this supreme positive law. It does not go beyond that to empower judges to enforce natural law.

Nor should it do so. The natural law enforced by judges could only be natural law as seen by a majority of the Justices of the U.S. Supreme Court, to which court all lower courts are subordinate. It is equally true that natural law translated into positive law by the sovereign people or their elected representatives can only be natural law as they understand it (and anyone who thinks that they are infallible has not been reading the newspapers recently). But the people can at least claim that under the Constitution they, and not the Supreme Court, are sovereign, and that the Constitution is their law, not the Court's.

Natural law must be translated into positive law through the medium of some group's conscience, to which conscience those of us who believe in natural law must appeal. I for one have more confidence in the long-term effectiveness of appealing to the conscience of the people—not a great deal of confidence, I must admit, but certainly more than I have in appealing to the conscience of our legal elite.

To illustrate my reason for this, a few years ago I gave a lecture to a student organization in the law school of a Catholic university. In my talk I argued vigorously against the Supreme Court's growing habit of finding rights not mentioned in the Constitution in the words "liberty" and "equal protection" in section 1 of the Fourteenth Amendment. The law faculty who attended disliked this argument intensely. One of them, a retired federal judge, got so angry that he asked, "Why should we be bound today by a document written two hundred years ago by people who are long since dead?" I answered, "Because that document is the only source of the authority of the Supreme Court." He and the rest of the faculty present laughed, and he exclaimed, "The only source of the authority of the Court is that the American people put up with it!" To this we have come: the Supreme Court is now a secular Holy See, and the law school professors are its theologians. The professors, at any rate, seem to think so.

For by far the greater part, the Supreme Court has assumed this role only in the present century and through its interpretation of the above-mentioned section 1 of the Fourteenth Amendment. The two clauses of that section which have served as the source of the Court's ever-expanding power are: "No State shall . . . deprive any person of life, liberty, or property, without due process of law"; or "deny to any person within its jurisdiction the equal protection of the laws." Since there is a parallel due process clause in the Fifth Amendment, the Court can and sometimes has used it to impose on the federal government the same restrictions that it finds imposed on the states by the equal protection clause.

The essential step in the Court's assumption of power has been to interpret "liberty" and "equality" (taken to be the meaning of "equal protection") as substantive rights whose content the Court may specify and apply to the decision of cases in constitutional law. Since the terms are broad and unspecified, the Court supplies their meaning case by case.

Nor could it be otherwise when the Court takes upon itself the task of determining and applying in precise legal terms the meaning of concepts as vague as liberty and equality. The Court finds the words in the Fourteenth Amendment, to be sure, but it does not find in the amendment any clear indication of their substantive meaning, with a mandate to specify that meaning and make it part of the supreme law of the land. By giving itself that mandate, the Court has made itself what it said in 1873 it did not want to be, a perpetual censor upon all the legislation of the states.[6] As Leonard W. Levy has said, "The states in our federal system can scarcely act without raising a Fourteenth Amendment question."[7] The Court decides the question.

Judge Bork has stated a much more restrained view of the due process clause: "The guarantee of due process . . . is simply a requirement that the substance of any law be applied to a person through fair procedures by any tribunal hearing a case. The clause says nothing about what the substance of the law must be." Substantive due process, he says, "transforms this requirement of fair procedures into a rule about the allowable substance of a statute."[8] But such a rule, whether the Justices care to admit it or not, is the incorporation of some concept of natural law (or justice, or right) into the Constitution, by judges and not by the authors of the law.

The common objection to this purely procedural interpretation of due process of law (and of equal protection) is that, if it were accepted, government, state governments in particular, could enact all manner of unjust and oppressive laws. So indeed they might and sometimes would. But those who want a Supreme Court that can remedy all injustices should take a hard look at the highly individualistic ethic that has informed so many of the Court's decisions since the 1960s, and ask themselves if that is the kind of natural law they want the Court to enforce.

Those who reject purely procedural due process fall roughly into three groups. There are liberals who favor government regulation of the economy, under the interstate commerce clause, for example, but want no governmental regulation of sexual conduct; they therefore defend "the right of privacy," as protecting conduct which they define as purely private. Economic liberals, commonly called conservatives in this country, may or may not want to protect "privacy," but emphatically want to protect property rights and private enterprise; but they largely lost that battle during the New Deal, when the Court admitted that "freedom of contract" was not in the Constitution. Finally, there are "social conservatives," who uphold laws that embody traditional morality, but they might appeal to the courts to invalidate laws contrary to that morality—laws, for example, that infringe upon the rights of society's basic institution, the family. Given the individualistic bias now built into our constitutional law, however, the social conservatives cannot expect much help from the courts. On the issue of abortion, the most the social conservatives could hope for from the Supreme Court would be for it to bow out of the struggle by reversing *Roe v. Wade*, and leave the issue to be resolved through the political process in the several states.

By striving to resolve great issues of public policy through Court interpretation of "liberty" and "equality," advocates of substantive due process politicize the judicial process and turn it into another way of getting what they were unable to get from the legislature. They thereby undermine judicial review because the more that people come to understand that constitutional law is politics carried on by other means, the less faith they have in the judiciary's impartiality and concern for the Constitution. As Justice White has said, "The Court is most vulnerable and comes nearest to illegitimacy when it deals with judge-made constitutional law having little or no cognizable roots in the language or design of the Constitution." For it is then that "the Judiciary takes to itself further authority to govern the country without express constitutional authority."[9] The higher the Court raises the stakes by engaging in this kind of law-making, the more intense the political struggles in which it involves itself. The bitterly fought battles we have seen in recent years over nominations to the Supreme Court are a direct result of the politicization of the judicial process.

Justice White's words of caution deserve to be heeded, no matter what good we may hope to accomplish by urging the Court to enforce rights not specified in the Constitution. For the Constitution is not a statement of a political philosophy, such as we find in the "self-evident truths" of the Declaration of Independence. Such a philosophy was necessary there to justify the extralegal and revolutionary act of renouncing what had hitherto been recognized as the legitimate authority of the King and Parliament of Great Britain. But the Constitution is not the justification of a revolution. It is a positive law made by a sovereign people in the exercise of the authority they had won by the American Revolution.

But, it is argued, the generation that wrote and ratified the Constitution is the same generation that wrote the Declaration of Independence and won the Revolution; we must therefore take the framers of the Constitution as having written it in the light of the philosophy of the Declaration. So they did, but not by giving judges the right to decide cases by direct appeals to natural law or natural rights.

The framers wrote a constitution that served the purposes enunciated in the Declaration. In that document, they created a federal government, and divided it into three branches that would check each other and so keep any one of them from monopolizing power and becoming despotic. They further protected the people's rights and liberties by conferring on this government only certain enumerated and limited powers.

When Anti-Federalists, who really did not want this new Constitution, objected to it on the ground that it did not contain a Bill of Rights, the Federalists who advocated ratification of the document replied that the Constitution was in itself a Bill of Rights: all powers that the people did not give to the government in the Constitution were rights that the people had reserved to themselves or to their state governments. In our constitutional system, it must be understood, a constitutional right is nothing more or less than a power denied to government; the refusal to give the power constitutes the right.

Nonetheless, since a number of states, in ratifying the Constitution, had expressed the wish that a Bill of Rights be added to it, James Madison proposed a list of explicit restraints on the federal government. They eventually became what we now call the Bill of Rights, i.e., the first ten amendments to the Constitution. To answer the Federalist criticism that listing some restrictions on the powers of the federal government might be taken to imply that these were the only restrictions, the Ninth Amendment was added.

It states that "the enumeration in the Constitution of certain rights shall not be construed to deny or disparage others retained by the people." That is to say that the explicit restrictions on federal power in the first eight amendments are not to be taken as the only ones. The rights "retained by the people" in the Ninth Amendment are simply all the powers that the people did not give to the federal government. They are not an amorphous mass of unspecified natural rights that courts may enforce.

The Tenth Amendment reemphasizes the point by stating: "The powers not delegated to the United States by the Constitution, nor prohibited by it to the States, are reserved to the States respectively, or to the people." Undelegated powers are the people's rights as against the *national* government. Constitutionally, they are nothing else. As for the states, they do not get their powers from the U.S. Constitution, but from their own people through their state constitutions, limited only by such prohibitions as the national Constitution imposes on them.

The Supreme Court may, and indeed must, declare federal laws unconstitutional when they are exercises of powers not delegated to the government by the Constitution. In that way the Court defends the rights of the people. But it may not take the Ninth Amendment as a grab bag of unspecified rights to be upheld against the federal government whenever a majority of its members thinks that justice requires it. To go farther and take the Ninth Amendment as giving the Court authority to maintain unspecified rights against the states, as some writers have done, borders on sheer intellectual dishonesty.

The question under the Constitution is not whether our government is bound by natural law and natural justice, but which organ of government is given authority to exercise its legal powers in the light of natural law. It is Congress that has that authority. Granted, the authority of Congress is limited; it may enact only those laws which the Constitution gives it the power to enact. But within that limit it may, for example, enact regulations of interstate commerce because it thinks them right and just, or even because it believes that they protect and promote the natural and inalienable rights of life, liberty, and the pursuit of happiness which the Declaration of Independence proclaims as the God-given ends of government. We may believe, for example, that Congress did just that in the Civil Rights Act of 1964, which it enacted under the interstate commerce clause (always, of course, remembering that, as John Bright said of the British Parliament, Congress sometimes does a good thing, but never merely because it is a good thing).

But consider what we should have agreed to if we accepted the power of the Supreme Court to use the rights to life, liberty, and the pursuit of happiness as rules of constitutional law. We should have conferred upon that eminent body the power to strike down as unconstitutional any law, federal or state, which in the opinion of a majority of the Justices impaired a plaintiff's life, liberty, or pursuit of happiness, and this without any specification in the text of what those words mean for the decision of a case. The constitutional authority to do that would be unlimited and arbitrary power, and that it might occasionally be exercised for a good end would not change that fact.

The Supreme Court has never claimed the power to enforce the Declaration of Independence or, for that matter, the Preamble to the Constitution. Yet, if it had done so and had gotten away with it, its power would differ very little from the one it now exercises through the substantive concepts of due process and equal protection. It is, of course, true that every constitutional limitation on the powers of legislatures and executives is ipso facto a grant of power to the courts. It must be so if the courts are to uphold the Constitution. But the Supreme Court itself is under the Constitution, not above it, and will remain there only if it remembers that the Constitution is a positive law, and not a grant of power to the Court to enact natural law or its own conceptions of natural right and justice. The latter power belongs in the first instance to the people, who ratified and can change the Constitution, and then to their elected representatives when they act within the boundaries of the powers conferred on them by the people.

The late Justice Hugo Black was commonly thought of in his day as a liberal. Yet he dissented strongly from the decision of the Supreme Court in the case of *Griswold v. Connecticut*[10] in which the Court struck down a Connecticut anticontraceptive law. That law, it held, violated "a right of privacy," which the Court admitted was not mentioned in the Constitution nor in the Bill of Rights, but which it claimed was implicit in the interstices of the Bill of Rights, and therefore in the substance of "liberty" in the Fourteenth Amendment. For good measure, the Court added the Ninth Amendment as a source of unspecified limitations on state powers.

Justice Black was the Court's strongest advocate of the idea that the Fourteenth Amendment was intended to make the Bill of Rights binding on the states as well as on the federal government. But what he liked about the Bill of Rights was that it was a list of specific and enumerated restraints on government, of the kind that a court could recognize and apply, and not a grant of virtually legislative power to the Supreme Court.

The essence of his dissent was that such a power could only be a usurped power:

> If any broad, unlimited power to hold laws unconstitutional because they offend what this Court conceives to be the "[collective] conscience of our people" is vested in this Court by the Ninth Amendment, the Fourteenth Amendment, or any other provision of the Constitution, it was not given by the Framers, but rather has been bestowed on the Court by the Court. . . . Use of any such broad unbounded judicial authority would make of this Court's members a day-to-day constitutional convention.

"The adoption of such a loose, flexible, uncontrolled standard for holding laws unconstitutional," he warned, ". . . will amount to a great unconstitutional shift of power to the courts," and this, he believed, "will be bad for the courts and worse for the country."[11]

That great unconstitutional shift of power to the courts has proceeded apace since Justice Black wrote those words. It would therefore be well if all of us stopped striving to realize objectives, however noble and good, by persuading the Court that it can find them in what Justice Felix Frankfurter once called "the vague contours of due process of law." For to the extent that we succeed we pervert judicial review and damage our constitutional system of government. That is indeed bad for the courts and worse for the country.

Notes

1. *The Works of the Right Honourable Edmund Burke*, 16 vols. (London: Rivington, 1803–27) 3: 144–45.

2. *Writings and Speeches of Edmund Burke*, set not yet complete (Oxford: Clarendon Press, 1981–   ) 2: 235.

3. (New York: Free Press, 1990), 66.

4. "Deconstructing the Constitution," *Academic Questions* 2 (1988–89): 13.

5. 1 Cranch 137, 176.

6. *The Slaughterhouse Cases*, 16 Wallace 36, 78.

7. "Foreword," in Howard Jay Graham, *Everyman's Constitution* (Madison: State Historical Society of Wisconsin, 1968), vii.

8. *The Tempting of America*, 31.

9. *Bowers v. Hardwick*, 478 U.S. 186, 194 (1986).

10. 381 U.S. 479 (1965).

11. Ibid., 520–21.

7

The Pluralist Game

The United States is a pluralist society. That is a commonplace and is taken as stating the problem to which the American relation between religion and the law is supposed to furnish the solution. The general principle of that relationship is an official government neutrality among all creeds, one that respects all beliefs but grants no favor to any of them. The name of the game is pluralism and the rules of the game can be summed up in one word: neutrality.

Unfortunately, however, our pluralism keeps changing. Today's pluralism is no longer that of even a quarter of a century ago. As the divisions on matters of fundamental belief become more and more pronounced in our society, the principle of neutrality becomes more difficult to apply to it.

As recently as 1960, the late John Courtney Murray, S.J., described the religion clauses of the First Amendment as "the twin children of social necessity, the necessity of creating a social environment, protected by law, in which men of differing faiths might live together in peace."[1] The faiths did indeed differ, and that fact constituted a political problem. It was also true, however, that all of the religions that had adherents numerous enough to matter shared a common Judeo-Christian tradition. Moreover, it was the respects in which they were substantially the same, namely, their moral teachings, that were politically significant and made the living together of their followers in peace a practical possibility. Now we must take notice of the fact that the differences both in faith and morals are steadily becoming deeper.

"Disintegration is the defining experience of the culture of modernism," a young professor at the Harvard Law School has written.[2] This

Law and Contemporary Problems (1981)

was, to be sure, a somewhat delphic statement, but a few quotations from other writers will suggest what he meant by it.

"One of the reasons why the novel has suffered so many strange mutations this century," an English literary critic has remarked, "is simply that the old shared assumptions about the nature of reality—the way of things, the why of things—have broken down. Increasingly, people are left bewildered at the workings of the world around them."[3] An important reason for this breakdown is the increasingly successful struggle of the individual self to free itself from the constraint of social norms.[4] According to the American critic Lionel Trilling, the "particular concern of the literature of the past two centuries has been with the self in its standing quarrel with culture."[5]

A group of sociologists give a more detailed explanation of the breakdown:

> Modern identity is *peculiarly Individuated*. The individual, the bearer of identity as the ens realissimum, quite logically attains a very important place in the hierarchy of values. Individual freedom, individual autonomy and individual rights come to be taken for granted as moral imperatives of fundamental importance, and foremost among these individual rights is the right to plan and fashion one's life as freely as possible. This basic right is elaborately legitimated by a variety of modern ideologies.[6]

This view of the individual and his rights has found its way even into the opinions of the U.S. Supreme Court, as this passage from the pen of the late Justice William Douglas reveals:

> Many of [the rights referred to in the Ninth Amendment] in my view come within the meaning of the term "liberty" as used in the Fourteenth Amendment.
> *First is the autonomous control over the development and expression of one's intellect, interests, tastes, and personality.*
> These are rights protected by the First Amendment and in my view they are absolute, permitting of no exceptions.[7]

Admittedly, Justice Douglas was as thoroughgoing an individualist as ever sat on the nation's highest bench, and he wrote the above words in a concurring opinion in which no other Justice joined him. Nonetheless, the attitude he expressed permeates contemporary American society and is shared by many who could not tell the Ninth Amendment from the First but are convinced that the Constitution endows them with an armory of absolute rights.

What follows from this degree of individualism has been pointed out by Iredell Jenkins: "Our skepticism regarding judgments of moral value springs from the fact that we are uneasy about what man should be; the ideas of freedom and equality have seduced us into accepting the doctrine of the ultimacy of the individual, with the result that every man becomes the sole judge of his own good."[8]

A handful of quotations such as these of itself proves nothing, of course. But it would be easy to fill a book with passages taken from a wide range of publications that reveal a growing awareness that the moral and intellectual consensus on which our society has lived is disintegrating. There is a widely diffused feeling that we are ceasing to agree even in basic respects on what man should be and how he should live. In consequence, much to the distress of politicians and political commentators, moral issues are being injected into law and politics that they would prefer to keep out. But given the nature of American pluralism today, it is hard to see how they can be kept out or how our traditional response to "divisive" issues can continue to work.

For we are no longer a pluralist society composed of a multitude of religious branches that sprang from a common stem. Lush as the variety of creeds in America has always been, by far the greater part of them held the Bible in common and in most respects taught substantially the same moral code. Historians will be quick to point out how large the number of the unchurched was even in colonial times, how soon the influence of the Enlightenment made itself felt on these shores, and how much indifferentism and outright skepticism coexisted almost from the beginning with religious faith. They are right, too, but only up to a point.

There never was a religious Golden Age in this country, or in any other for that matter. Nor was there ever a static period in which the religious situation in America stood still for decades. But recognition of these facts should not blind us to the extent to which a common religious and moral tradition perdured through centuries of change and fragmentation. As late as 1931 the U.S. Supreme Court could declare: "We are a Christian people. . . ."[9] It is a measure of the distance we have come in the last half-century that one cannot imagine the Court saying that today.

Our pluralism has increased and is increasing. This is, to be sure, a not unexpected development. It means only that a profound cultural shift that began centuries ago on the other side of the Atlantic has finally eroded what remained of the earlier religious and moral tradition in the minds of multitudes of Americans. It has incidentally also left millions of other Americans with the feeling that they are now strangers in their own land. Today we are forced to ask whether the picture of an impartial state presiding with what Chief Justice Warren Burger has called "benevolent neutrality"[10] over the peaceful coexistence of a multitude of sects still fits the facts to a serviceable degree. In the face of the new pluralism that is emerging we must inquire how realistic is the ideal of neutrality as we have understood it up to now.

The neutral state, as we have inherited it, is the liberal state. The historical genesis of liberalism and the state it formed is no simple thing. It was the product of many factors, and what they were and how they interacted is a matter of considerable dispute among scholars. But for our present purpose it is safe to say that liberalism was a response to the situation created by two great movements, the Reformation and the Enlightenment. One of these replaced the unity of medieval Christendom with a multiplicity of churches. The other, as Lester G. Crocker has put it, was "the beginning of the godless age,"[11] in which Christianity in any form eventually ceased to be the common religion of Western culture.

An early response to the religious divisions that followed the Reformation was crystallized in the phrase *cujus regio, ejus religio.* That is to say, the government of a country would determine its religion and require all inhabitants to conform to it. But since this policy, far from ending strife, made control of the government an object to be gained by armed force, the solution that eventually prevailed was to take religion out of politics.

Doing this did not necessarily require a formal "separation of Church and State" such as was established in the United States by the First Amendment. Great Britain has shown that a formal religious establishment can become compatible with a high degree of religious liberty. But it did require that a man's freedom to follow his own religion or no religion should not be denied or seriously burdened by governmental action.

Freedom of religion was but one instance of liberalism's instinct for taking neuralgic issues out of politics. Liberal politics must be confined to matters of secondary importance like war and taxes (curious as it may sound to say that) because bitterly though citizens may disagree about these things, they do not usually take up arms against each other about them as they did over religion. Not only religious issues, however, but all issues that engender more emotion than the political system can bear must be excluded from politics. Preeminent among these are moral issues, because they both deeply affect the way people live and are closely connected with their more general fundamental beliefs, be these religious or secularist.

Liberal government therefore is neutral government. But to make this assertion only raises the question: neutral about what? The answer to that question turns out to be itself a political and even a moral issue. Robert Dahl, for example, has discussed a number of ways in which people who believe in political equality, and therefore in democracy, may yet protect themselves against majority decisions which they regard as overbearing and oppressive. One of them is this:

> Sometimes a matter about which we disagree can be turned over so completely to the domain of personal choice that no generally binding decision is required. Two familiar issues of this kind are the religious instruction, if any, to be given one's own children and whether they are to be educated in public or private schools. A few years ago the Supreme Court of the United States affirmed that the use of contraceptive devices falls in this domain. One might call this alternative a solution by Autonomous Decisions.[12]

We may thus seem to have an answer to our question. Government should be neutral about matters that belong in the area of Autonomous Decisions. But Dahl immediately points out that the boundaries of this area are themselves a subject of continuing controversy:

> Judgments as to the appropriate domain of Autonomous Decisions are constantly changing. Efforts to define the domain once and for all have always failed. Thus in the United States, owning and driving a machine that emits exhaust fumes is rapidly moving out of the domain of Autonomous Decisions to regulation by collective decision. . . , while sexual practices among consenting adults are moving from collective regulation to the domain of individual choice.[13]

Even more important is the following consideration:

> To be sure, once we have agreed that a particular matter belongs within the domain of Autonomous Decisions, the possibility of conflict between minority and majority is eliminated with respect to that matter. But to determine what remains in or out of the domain of this kind is often a source of very profound conflict. . . . What properly belongs within the domain of Autonomous Decisions or Consumers' Choice has been a perpetual point of controversy between majorities and minorities.[14]

What belongs in the area of Autonomous Decisions is, therefore, a question that requires a public and political decision. In making such a decision the people, through their representatives, take a public stand on what they will leave to individual choice and what they will subject to legal regulation. Leaving a matter to individual choice is as much a public decision as deciding to regulate it and implies some public scheme of values quite as much as a decision to regulate does.

In practice, of course, the controversy over a question of this kind gets such settlement as it does get through a political process in which expediency and rhetoric play a large part. Slogans such as "You can't legislate morality" and "No group has a right to impose its morality on others" are freely used. If at all possible, the First Amendment is invoked on the absolute necessity of separating church and state. In fact, however, the size and (perhaps even more important) the financial power of the groups involved, and the importance that both sides attach to the values at stake, have more to do with the way in which the dispute is settled than does any appeal to principle.

The American people in the nineteenth century felt few qualms about banning polygamy throughout the United States, even though John Stuart Mill had warned them against doing so in Utah. Since the Mormons had exiled themselves to a remote and previously uninhabited territory in order to practice polygamy, he said, "it is difficult to see on what principles but those of tyranny they can be prevented from living there under what laws they please, provided they commit no aggression on other nations and allow perfect freedom of departure to those who are dissatisfied with their ways."[15] But the Mormons were few in number and without influence, while on the other hand monogamy was solidly embedded in the religious and moral beliefs of the great majority of Americans.

The U.S. Supreme Court, as was fitting in a First Amendment case, found a secular and political reason for upholding the federal law against the practice of polygamy in the territories. The Court declared that "polygamy leads to the patriarchal principle, . . . which, when applied to large communities, fetters the people in stationary despotism, while the principle cannot long exist in connection with monogamy."[16] The ban on polygamy, according to the Court, struck a blow for political liberty. One may suspect, however, that the Court was in fact reflecting the moral conscience of the people at large.

Conversely, one may suspect that if the polygamous minority were not so small—if, say, 45 percent of Americans believed in polygamy and many of them wanted to practice it—the Supreme Court (today's if not yesterday's) would find polygamy to be in the domain of Autonomous Decisions or, as the Court prefers to put it, to be included in the right of privacy. The Court would of course also have to try to gauge the feelings of the 55 percent majority who still objected to polygamy. How strong are their feelings? Will the majority swallow a flat declaration that prohibiting polygamy is beyond the constitutional powers of government? Or must we take a more gradual approach by finding one antipolygamy statute after another vague and overbroad while maintaining that in principle government may regulate polygamy? These would be difficult and delicate questions to answer. But one way or another, the Court, along with other agencies of government, would search for a means of taking the divisive issue of polygamy out of politics.

The reason for doing so would be the practical one of lessening social and political strife. The principle justification for doing it, however, would be the neutrality among conflicting beliefs to which government is committed in a liberal society. But the justification would only raise once again the questions of the matters about which government ought to be neutral, how far it should go in the quest for neutrality, and to what extent neutrality is ultimately possible.

We must admit that a liberal society has a permanent bias in favor of neutrality. The liberal state is founded on no such vision of human excellence as informed the political theories of Plato and Aristotle, no such hope of earthly and eternal happiness as inspired the medieval *res publica Christiana*. The liberal state aims only at equal liberty for all under impartial general laws. The use that men make of their liberty and the goals they pursue are for them to decide. Any attempt by society or its agent, the state, to make the decision for them must be rejected as an effort by some citizens to impose their conception of excellence, virtue, or happiness on others.

The liberal state therefore aims low and attempts only to establish the conditions of ordered liberty in which men can peacefully pursue their essentially private ends. Such a state obviously never existed in its pure form. The laissez-faire state of the nineteenth century was probably the closest approach to it in actuality. It must also be remembered that the implications of the liberal view of man as a naturally sovereign individual motivated by his subjective concept of his own interest were worked out only very gradually over a period of several centuries. Liberalism reached its apogee in the Victorian era when it could still be assumed that ladies and gentlemen had a common code of manners and even of morals, and when one could still hope—with whatever misgivings—to civilize the masses through popular education and good literature. The proposal to free the individual to follow his preferences and to choose his own way of living took certain built-in checks for granted. It is only today that we begin fully to understand what liberal individualism really implies.

The liberal ideal of governmental neutrality ought to require (and in the nineteenth century was thought to require) a minimalist conception of the state. A state that aims at achieving neutrality by leaving to private choice those matters on which beliefs and values differ should try to do as little as possible. When it does act, it should do so only in areas of common material concern about which general agreement can be assumed, e.g., paving the streets and providing protection against fires. When it finds it necessary to intervene in matters that transcend the merely material, it should help people to carry out their own decisions rather than decide for them.

Thus for example, if it is judged that a liberal democracy needs an educated citizenry, the state should not run schools but should content itself with obliging parents to send their children to school and should provide them with the means of doing so if that is necessary. For, as John Stuart Mill remarked in 1859, "a general State education is a mere contrivance for molding people to be exactly like one another" and "establishes a despotism over the mind, leading by natural tendency to one over the body."[17]

It is true that Mill later changed his mind on this point, and that is not surprising. He was, after all, one of the heralds of the shift in liberal thought that took place around the turn of this century and led to the welfare-state liberalism of the present age. With the advent of the welfare state, the problem of governmental neutrality clearly becomes more acute. A state that acts vigorously on a number of fronts to promote people's welfare must have some idea of what their welfare is. That necessarily implies some conception of what is good for human beings and what is bad for them. Having such a conception, the state cannot pretend to be neutral about it.

One can, to be sure, defend the neutrality of welfare liberalism by asserting that the welfare state does no more than try to guarantee to all citizens the minimum conditions in which they may effectively pursue their private goals. In a modern society, the individual needs a basic education, a place in which to live, a job to give him an income, and a pension to support him in old age. Government does not abandon neutrality by taking action to ensure that he has these things, for it leaves him completely free to think, say, read, and view what he pleases, and to act on any life-plan that does not violate the rights of others.

Preserving this kind of neutrality in a welfare state turns out, however, to be somewhat more difficult than welfare liberals care to admit.

The difficulty is most obvious in education because of its inevitable intellectual and moral content, though it by no means appears only there. Forty years ago Alexander Meiklejohn pointed out the problem when he asked whether the public schools of New York had any view of life to teach: "Does New York City believe anything? Has it any values or convictions out of which a scheme of teaching may be made?"[18]

Does New York City believe anything? One answer to that question, an answer that seems to find favor with the U.S. Supreme Court, is: No, but New York can still educate. Public education, as Justice Brennan once explained, consists solely in imparting skills and factual information.[19] These constitute objective knowledge that is value-free and neutral in content. New York, therefore, or any other city can teach them from no particular point of view and without believing anything about life.

The premise of this position, however, is a distinction between facts and values, between scientific "knowledge" and religious, philosophical, or ethical "faith." But this distinction itself derives from a particular, sectarian, and today much-controverted theory of the nature of knowledge. Its name is positivism, and one can hardly maintain that positivism is now universally accepted in informed and intelligent circles. To make it the premise of a theory of education, therefore, is not neutrality.

Furthermore, it is questionable whether Justice Brennan's view accurately describes what public schools actually do. These schools today teach children about subjects as diverse as sex and citizenship, history and histology, law and literature. All of them are no doubt worthy subjects of study. But it requires some exercise of the imagination to believe that they can be taught merely as sets of objective facts, without value judgments and without implying criteria of evaluation, decision, and action.

The sincere effort at neutrality would seem to defeat itself. To teach children, for example, that they have interesting and complementary sexual anatomies, but that the teacher, being neutral, can say no more about the proper use of them than that there are differing schools of thought on the question, appears likely to tilt the balance in favor of regarding sexual conduct as simply a matter of taste and preference, of no social consequence so long as precautions are taken against unwanted offspring. Many people today, operating through well-financed organizations (often, in fact, federally financed), do advocate that view and try to propagate it in the schools. But siding with them is presumably not what we mean by neutrality.

One can state the problem in more general terms. Decisions on public policy concern the use of means to achieve social goals. In a society where a strong consensus on the general goals of policy exists, the decisions need not concern anything other than the choice of means to the agreed-upon goals. The goals in turn are agreed upon because they derive from a prevailing view of the nature of man, of what is good for him and of what his basic social relations ought to be. As consensus on these matters breaks down, the choice not only of means but also of ends becomes a subject of controversy, and this fact cannot be indefinitely obscured by appeals to the neutrality of the state and the equality of citizens under the law.

Affirmative action programs, for example, are designed to promote equality. But they rest upon largely unexamined and uncriticized assumptions about the nature of the equality to be promoted. The most basic of these assumptions is the conception, inherited from seventeenth- and eighteenth-century social contract theories, of mankind as a multitude of autonomous individual subjects of rights whose relations with one another and with society are voluntary and contractual. This conception today underlies the picture of the adult and adolescent population of the United States as made up of actual or potential jobholders who may, if they wish, marry and raise children as an avocation, but whose equal access to jobs without distinction by race, sex, creed, or sexual preference is the overriding concern of the law.

The point being made here is not that this theory of equality is false, but merely that it is neither demonstrably true nor universally accepted. The exercise of human intelligence does not automatically and necessarily commit us to so radically individualistic a view of human nature or to the kind of equality that follows from it. Still believing in the basic equality of all human beings, it would be possible to conceive of man in more communitarian terms and to think of men and women as persons whose relations flow from their complementary sexual natures. In this view, differentiation of social roles that took sex into account would make sense.

Let us push the matter a little farther. The principle that the state may deny to no person the equal protection of the laws has not been understood to forbid all legal classifications but only those which are arbitrary and unreasonable. But what is reasonable? The classic liberal answer was that the allocation of social status and rewards on the basis of merit, but on no other basis, was reasonable. A man has a right to what he has earned, disproportionate though it may be to what others get, but he has a right to no more. But, as Roberto Mangabeira Unger points out, in a liberal society, belief in meritocracy itself eventually comes under attack:

> Every conventional criterion for the allocation of social advantages falls under the suspicion that it, too, is arbitrary. Even reliance on merit becomes suspect when its dependence on the distribution of genetic endowments is taken into account, for people may begin to doubt whether a man's social place should be determined by a fact of which he is not the author.[20]

One may indeed ask why he should be expected to go to the end of the line when the good things of life are distributed, merely because he was born to poor, culturally deprived, and perhaps genetically inferior parents. Followed all the way through, Yves Simon explained, this line of questioning leads to the conclusion that all children should be taken from their parents at birth and raised in state nurseries, lest one child be more "advantaged" than another.[21] Given today's biological technology, one can dream of the day when children will not be born at all but will come out of genetic blenders in state hatcheries, so that no child will be even genetically superior to another.

Simon's answer to this line of argument was that we limit the principle of equality of opportunity when it begins to destroy the very things for which we wanted opportunity in the first place: "A policy of equal opportunity begins to be harmful when it threatens to dissolve the small communities [primarily the family] from which men derive their best energies in the hard accomplishments of daily life."[22]

But Simon belonged to the school of philosophical realism and believed in an objectively real common nature of man. He was, in fact, a Thomist, therefore a sectarian. Yet the opposing and ultimately nominalist school of thought is fully as sectarian. All doctrines of equality rest upon some philosophy and some conception of the nature of man. No state can promote equality without consciously or unconsciously, explicitly or implicitly, adopting one view or another. It has been the genius of the liberal pluralist society to avoid raising such questions of fundamental philosophy as far as possible. But as the issues that surface in debates on public policy become more profound, avoiding these questions becomes correspondingly less possible. Pretending that they can be dealt with by plain, blunt common sense without resort to premises of a higher level is at best a refusal to face the issues. At worst, it is an effort to play the pluralist game with a stacked deck.

Shifting the issues over to the area of autonomous decisions also proves to be no escape. The U.S. Supreme Court tried to do this with the abortion issue in *Roe v. Wade*[23] and subsequent cases by holding that the right to decide on an abortion belongs only to the expectant mother, advised by her physician, without interference by the state, her husband, or her parents. Thus, it was alleged, the state achieved neutrality on the subject of abortion: no woman could by law be required to have an abortion or prevented from having one, since the Constitution as interpreted left the decision to her alone.

The import of this holding has at times been exaggerated. For instance, Chief Circuit Judge Clement Haynsworth, speaking for a three-judge federal court, has said that ''the Supreme Court declared the fetus in the womb is neither alive nor a person within the meaning of the Fourteenth Amendment.''[24] But it is doubtful if the Supreme Court claimed a power that God Himself might envy, that of making a live fetus dead merely by declaring it so. The Court's decision, rather, was an assertion, not that the fetus lacked life, but that the value to be attached to its life was only what its mother chose to give it. If she wanted a baby, its prenatal life was a value which the state could protect but only because she wanted it. If she did not want a child to be born, its life could be destroyed by abortion. That is to say, at least for the first two trimesters, its life had no intrinsic value that the state could recognize and protect independently of the will of the mother.

The Court therefore did not really achieve neutrality by making abortion a matter of private choice immune from public control. Instead, it committed the United States to a value judgment on prenatal life. The same question will arise in regard to postnatal life when, as seems likely, euthanasia becomes a constitutional issue. According to the *New York Times,* it has already become the subject of ''an emotional debate in Britain'' occasioned by the publication of a booklet entitled ''How to Die with Dignity'' that described various methods of suicide. This debate, the *Times* reported, centered on the questions, ''Is there a 'right to commit suicide,' as basic as the right to live? And if there is, is it proper to help people to kill themselves, either actively or by advising them?''[25]

The issue thus posed is both basic and unavoidable. The person whose life is to be terminated by euthanasia wants to die. He therefore claims the right to end his life, or to have it ended by a doctor, on the premise that the only value of life is a purely subjective one, and his life is no longer of value to him. The argument against letting him choose death—when all subsidiary and distracting arguments about fully informed consent have been settled—must invoke the principle that human life is a value in itself, an objective human good, that the state exists to protect. Faced with this issue, the U.S. Supreme Court could not pretend to be neutral by finding euthanasia to be included in the constitutional right of privacy, thus making life and death objects of private choice. So to decide would be to come down on one side of the controversy, that side which holds that life has only subjective value.

Similarly, arguments for recognition of the civil rights of homosexuals, to the extent that they are a demand for public acceptance of heterosexuality and homosexuality as separate but equal ways of life, pose an issue to which there is no neutral answer. This is a demand that the public commit itself to a particular view of the nature and function of sex in human life. Faced with this demand, the public and its government cannot take refuge in a specious neutrality by leaving the matter to individual consciences.

To do so would be a public declaration that in the eyes of society and its laws, sexual preferences are merely that—personal and subjective preferences of no objective validity and no public importance. That view may arguably be the correct one, but it is not a neutral refusal to hold any view at all. Nor, if adopted, would it succeed in relegating questions of sexual preference to the purely private domain.

Consider, for example, the case of *Belmont v. Belmont.* A divorced and remarried father applied in the New Jersey Superior Court for a change in the custody of his children from his former wife to himself on the ground that she was living in a lesbian relationship deleterious to the welfare of the children. According to the *Family Law Reporter,* the court "found him to be suitable as a custodian in all respects." Nonetheless, it rejected his application and ruled that "the mother is not to be denied custody merely because of her sexual orientation. Her sexual preference and her living arrangement with her lover are only two of the many factors to be examined in determining the best interest of the children."[26] In so ruling, the court committed the state of New Jersey to the proposition that a homosexual union is, or can be, as acceptable a one in which to raise children as is a heterosexual one dignified by matrimony. This is something more than a decision to leave sexual preferences up to individuals. It is a public stand in regard to the institution of the family.

Viewed from a certain angle, the ultimate liberal ideal appears to be normlessness. In its extreme form (which for some curious reason is now regarded as "conservative"), this ideal is called libertarianism. The most radical brand of libertarianism holds that there should be no social norms enforced by the state, and indeed no state to enforce them.

The only norms should be those that emerge from the consent of individuals who voluntarily join a variety of social groups. But all forms of liberalism, even the most statist, regard the ideal situation as one in which the individual freely—and, of course, intelligently—sets norms for himself. If regulation is necessary, as most liberals concede and even insist that it is, its ultimate justification is that it contributes to the individual's freedom to shape his life as he will.

Normlessness, however, turns out to be itself a norm. It is a steady choice of individual freedom over any other human or social good that conflicts with it, and unrelenting subordination of all allegedly objective goods to the subjective good of individual preference. Such a policy does not merely set individuals free to shape their own lives. It necessarily sets norms for a whole society, creates an environment in which everyone has to live, and exerts a powerful influence on social institutions.

This is particularly apparent in a welfare state where, for example, the argument is constantly urged that it is unjust to allow the rich and the middle class to do what the poor cannot afford to do. The first stage of argument is that the hand of the law must be withdrawn from an activity found to be included in the right of privacy. Once it has been established, however, that contraception, abortion, or divorce, for example, are little or no business of government, the argument moves into its second stage. These activities are now constitutional rights and, as such, are presented as positive claims on government. Those who cannot afford to engage in them with their own resources must be subsidized, so that they may exercise their constitutional rights as effectively as the more well-to-do. What was originally withdrawn from the power of government should now, we are told, become an object of government policy.

The U.S. Supreme Court, as we know, has refused to turn this argument into a constitutional command.[27] That does not change the fact that government is under constant pressure—to which it frequently yields—to use its power to promote or enforce new norms in the guise of leaving normative decisions to individuals. The net result is not no norms but different norms and a reshaping of the institutions of society.

A similar result would follow even in a classically liberal society that did not maintain a welfare state. Such a society would not subsidize the exercise of private rights but it would nonetheless have to make up its mind on the nature and content of the rights that it would recognize and protect. Merely by making this decision it would set social norms.

For example, Anglo-American law has always given a privileged position to the institution of marriage, and to a large though lesser extent it still does so. Marriage entails obligations and some of them are legally enforceable. But it also entails rights—economic as well as strictly marital and familial ones—that find a place in the law in a multitude of ways. Now the preferred position of marriage creates social norms. No other sexual relationship, even if tolerated by law, enjoys the same legal protection and consequent social prestige as marriage. The law discriminates systematically in favor of marriage.

In principle, a liberal society could rectify this discrimination. Doing so would require reducing marriage to the status of a private contract like any other, to be entered into and dissolved at will, subject only to the limitations created by the legitimate interests of other persons that may have arisen from the contract (the children will always be a problem in even the most liberal Garden of Eden). The content of the contract, of course, would have to be left to the contracting parties. It could include provisions for extramarital larks, ménages à trois, and homosexual as well as heterosexual unions. The only function of the state would be to enforce the contract while it lasted.

We must ask, however, whether a society that went that far in its quest for equal freedom for all would have eliminated discrimination and achieved neutrality. At first glance, it appears that it would have done so. Individuals would still be free to contract heterosexual, monogamous, and lifelong marriages, just as before, and the state would enforce these contracts, too. All that would have happened would be the removal of an invidious distinction in favor of one form of sexual union.

But to take this position is implicitly to assert that the only value of marriage is a purely private one. The best sexual relationship is the one that best pleases the individuals who participate in it. Their pleasure is the norm because no other norm is admissible. But accepting that proposition is not normlessness. It is the clear choice of one basic social norm over all others, a choice that has far-reaching consequence for all of society.

After all, the Supreme Court had a point when it said in the Mormon polygamy case in 1878: "Marriage, while from its very nature a sacred obligation, is, nevertheless, in most civilized nations, a civil contract, and usually regulated by law. Upon it society may be said to be built, and out of its fruits spring social . . . obligations and duties, with which government is necessarily required to deal."[28] Since marriage is a highly visible social fact, government must take some attitude toward it. To regard marriage and the family as the foundation of society, as the Court did in 1878, is to adopt a particular view of man and society.

This view inevitably becomes the basis of coercive laws, such as those which prohibit bigamy and polygamy. But it is an equally particular view of man and society to regard marriage and its alternatives as matters of purely private concern. If they are so regarded, then private decisions about them are entitled to protection from interference and infringement, for example, by laws to prevent landlords from refusing to rent apartments to couples who wish to cohabit without being married. Either way, some view concerning sexual relationships gets enforced by the power of law. What is impossible is to take no view at all and call it neutrality.

A pluralist society must perforce strive to be neutral about many things that concern its divided citizens. But it cannot be neutral about all of them. If it tries or pretends to be neutral about certain issues, the pluralist game becomes a shell game by which people are tricked into consenting to changes in basic social standards and institutions on the pretense that nothing more is asked of them than respect for the rights of individuals. Much more, however, is involved: on the fundamental issues of social life, one side or the other always wins.

To say this leaves unanswered the question, Which issues are of fundamental importance? That is a question that any given society will as a matter of fact decide for itself. The only point that need be made here is that a society may make this decision because it must make it. There is no way of avoiding decision since the ostensible refusal to decide is itself a decision.

Nor is there any neat line that can be drawn between political issues and moral issues, or between law and morality. As we have said, the decision to leave certain moral issues to individual choice is a public decision that reflects an underlying public moral judgment. Public decisions to leave certain matters to individual consciences may be and often are wise and right, but neutral they are not.

There is also no neat line that can be drawn between religion and morality. The state, under our Constitution, is not permitted to enforce the Ten Commandments on the ground that they have been revealed by God. On the other hand, the state is not barred from enforcing certain principles of the Ten Commandments for the reason that some of its citizens believe that they have been revealed by God. Which of the commandments may or should be enforced, to what extent they should be enforced, and by what legal means are open questions for public moral decision.

There is inescapably a public morality—a good one or a bad one—in the sense of some set or other of basic norms in the light of which the public makes policy decisions. These norms are moral norms to the extent that they include fundamental judgments on what is good or bad for human beings, therefore on what it is permissible or obligatory to do to them or for them. Public morality is a secular morality inasmuch as it aims only at secular goals, at the welfare of men in this world. It is not therefore a secularist morality. When discussing the welfare of human beings in the here and now we are not limited to the vision of man and his good that happens to be held by those who call themselves secular humanists. Secular humanism is not the least common denominator of all American beliefs about human welfare. It is but one sectarian view among many, and any American is free to believe that he derives from his religion a richer, fuller, and more truly human image of man. He is also free to use it as a basis for the views he advocates on public policy.

Leo Pfeffer has announced the Triumph of Secular Humanism, which he seems to regard as the resolution of the Issues That Divide.[29] That victory may or may not be a fact; one sometimes has the impression that the battle is not over yet. But if it proves to be the fact, we should at least not delude ourselves about what has happened. It will not be the advent of a truly neutral state but the replacement of one view of man, with the ethic and the legal norms based on it, by another view.[30]

In the meantime the Issues That Divide will continue to divide our people ever more deeply. The pluralist game will continue to be played, of course, because there is no other game in town. But there is no need for it to keep on being a confidence game in which one side proclaims its cause as neutrality and the other side is gullible enough to believe it. Societies do face moral issues to which they must give moral answers. The answers we arrive at through the political process in our pluralist society are likely to be rather messy, somewhat confused, and certainly less than universally satisfactory ones. Answers nonetheless will be arrived at, and they will have definite effects on our society. We shall play the pluralist game more honestly, perhaps even with better results, if we admit openly what the game is and what stakes we are playing for.

Notes

1. *We Hold These Truths: Catholic Reflections on the American Proposition* (New York: Sheed and Ward, 1960), 57.
2. Roberto Mangabeira Unger, *Knowledge and Politics* (New York: Free Press, 1975), 26.

3. Tony Tanner, "The Great American Nightmare," *The Spectator* 216 (1966): 530.

4. One of the best descriptions of this process is Philip Rieff, *The Triumph of the Therapeutic: Uses of Faith After Freud* (New York: Harper & Row, 1966).

5. Quoted in Elting E. Morison, ed., *The American Style* (New York: Harper, 1958), 196.

6. Peter Berger, Brigitte Berger, and Hansfried Kellner, *The Homeless Mind: Modernization and Consciousness* (New York: Random House, 1973), 79.

7. Concurring, *Doe v. Bolton*, 410 U.S. 179, 210–11 (1973).

8. Book review, *American Journal of Jurisprudence* 16 (1971): 316.

9. *U.S. v. Macintosh*, 283 U.S. 605, 625 (1931).

10. *Walz v. Tax Commission,* 397 U.S. 664, 669 (1970).

11. "Presidential Address" in Louis T. Milic, ed., *The Modernity of the Eighteenth Century* (Cleveland: Case Western Reserve University Press, 1971), xviii.

12. *After the Revolution? Authority in a Good Society* (New Haven: Yale University Press, 1970), 19.

13. Ibid., 19–20.

14. Ibid., 24–25.

15. *On Liberty* (Indianapolis: The Library of Liberal Arts, Bobbs-Merrill Co., 1956), 112–13.

16. *Reynolds v. U.S.* 98 U.S. 145, 166 (1878), citing Lieber, "The Mormons: Shall Utah be Admitted into the Union?" *Putnam's Monthly*, March 1855, 225.

17. *On Liberty*, 129, n. 15.

18. *Education Between Two Worlds* (New York: Harper & Bros., 1942), 5.

19. Concurring, *Lemon v. Kurtzman*, 403 U.S. 602, 655 (1971).

20. *Law in Modern Society: Toward a Criticism of Social Theory* (New York: Free Press, 1976), 172.

21. *Philosophy of Democratic Government* (Chicago: University of Chicago Press, 1951), 225.

22. Ibid., 228–29.

23. 410 U.S. 113 (1973).

24. *Floyd v. Anders*, 440 F. Supp. 535, 539 (D.S.C. 1977).

25. "Suicide Guide Stirs a Debate in Britain," *New York Times*, September 28, 1980, 7, col. 1.

26. *Belmont v. Belmont*, 6 FLR 2785–86 (N.J. Sup. 1980).

27. *Harris v. McRae*, 448 U.S. 297 (1980).

28. 98 U.S. 145, 165 (1878).

29. "Issues That Divide: The Triumph of Secular Humanism," *Journal of Church and State* 19 (1977): 203.

30. For a cold-bloodedly realistic assessment of what will be involved in this shift of views, see the editorial entitled "A New Ethic for Medicine and Society," *California Medicine* 113 (1970): 67.

8

The Problem of Belief in America

Crystal-ball gazing is a pleasant sport. But it is a risky one, because an effort to foretell and judge the future depends on a series of analyses of the present and of estimations of the shape of things to come. Any of these is open to attack by critics and to falsification by events. Yet one must take the risk and make certain assumptions if one is to talk intelligibly about the years that lie ahead. But both writer and reader should be aware that they are not simply thinking about reality, but are choosing interpretations of it.

With this caveat, then, let us discuss what it will mean to be a Catholic in America in the foreseeable future. One can take the word ''mean'' here in a double sense. It can refer to the social situation in which Catholics will live and which will enhance or diminish their ability to live out the implications of their faith. What one thinks it will mean to be Catholic in America, in this sense, depends on one's judgment on American society and on the major forces shaping its religious future. In another sense, the meaning of Catholicism is its intrinsic content. In this sense, what one sees as the meaning of being Catholic in the future depends on one's understanding of the Catholic Church and of the faith which it teaches.

Even to use these words is, of course, to prejudge the question. There are those who call themselves Catholics but who deny that one can any longer speak meaningfully of an institution called the Church, whose function is to teach a body of doctrine authoritatively, while the function of the institution's members is to believe what they are taught and to shape their lives in accordance with their beliefs. Such a conception

Communio (1975)

of the Church, these Catholics say, is a legacy of the past that we must abandon without regret.

The future belongs instead, they tell us, to communities of believers holding a stripped-down version of Christian faith and morals on which the members of today's divided churches can agree as they unite with one another in a consummation of the ecumenical movement. The meaning of being Catholic, therefore, must be subsumed into the more general meaning of being Christian. The question then will be the stance that an ecumenical Christianity should take toward America.

One may venture the guess that the members of this decentralized and nonauthoritative church of the future will have less difficulty in adjusting themselves to American society than will the members of the Catholic Church as we have known it. If the Catholic Church and the Catholic faith remain substantially what they have been—and that they will is the interpretation of reality chosen as the basis of this paper—the meaning of being Catholic will be clear enough. But it will be harder to make it compatible with being American, if certain observable developments in our society continue.

The first of these is neither recent nor peculiarly American. It is the de-Christianization of Western culture, and it has been going on for at least three centuries. As the late Crane Brinton wrote, in the latter part of the seventeenth century "there arose in our society what seems to me clearly to be a new religion, certainly related to, descended from and by many reconciled with, Christianity. I call this religion simply Enlightenment, with a capital E."[1] Whether the "new religion" of the Enlightenment can be reconciled with Christianity is still today a basic issue dividing Christians: the belief that a reconciliation is possible is the foundation of liberal or progressive Christianity. But the position adopted here is that the reconciliation is ultimately impossible.

When the Enlightenment flowered in the eighteenth century, its incompatibility with a Christian view of the world became clear. At least, that is a very common understanding of the movement, which a scholar has recently stated in these words:

> The eighteenth century was the beginning of the godless age, even though there were atheists before that century, and though most of its writers and thinkers were not atheists. But the God in which they believed became increasingly un-Christian, remote and vague. . . . In most matters of actual concern, be it science, politics, or morals, God became increasingly irrelevant. Whether or not men realized it, their thinking and their conduct were increasingly free from the feeling that He was there with them, looking at

them. Even more, there was for the first time a concerted attack not only against religion and theology but against God; for science, materialism, and ethics sought to free themselves from age-old shackles and to assume a completely independent, a completely human, responsibility.[2]

In this respect, as in others, the eighteenth was the first modern century. Only, what was shocking then has become familiar to us now. We have lived so long with de-Christianization that we accept it as an established fact and overlook it as a continuing trend. We take it for granted that we live in a pluralist society whose golden rule must be tolerance of the most diverse opinions. But today's pluralist society is not merely the result of the loss of faith by multitudes in the past. It is also an advanced stage on the way to a post-Christian secular culture.

Public opinion polls indicate that de-Christianization is less pronounced in the United States than in many countries of Western Europe, if we take the number of people who profess belief in heaven and hell as the criterion. But here as abroad belief in the immortality of the soul and the eternal destiny of man has waned. Men's view of the goals of life has consequently become secular, confined to this world alone. It is possible to believe, as the editors of *l'Encyclopédie* did in the 1750s and the editors of the *New York Times* still do, that we can build a rational and humane society on a purely secular worldview. But others have commented less optimistically on the implications of this enormous cultural change.

Irving Kristol, for example, has written: "I think it possible to suggest that the decline of the belief in personal immortality has been the most important political fact of the last hundred years—nothing else has so profoundly affected ways in which the masses of people experience their worldly condition."[3] It is, he believes, a major cause of the revolution of rising expectations that puts strains on political systems that they may not be able to stand.

A century ago, in his *Liberty, Equality, Fraternity*, James Fitzjames Stephen observed the decline of religious faith and pointed out some of its moral implications:

Suppose . . . it were to be established beyond all doubt whatever, that there is no life at all beyond the grave, and that this doctrine was accepted by the whole human race with absolute confidence. This would have an equally powerful and direct influence both on law and morals. The value which is set upon human life, especially upon the lives of the sick, the wretched, and superfluous children would at once appear to be exaggerated. Lawyers would have occasion to reconsider the law of murder, and especially the law of infanticide. . . .[4]

More recently a review of the writings of George Orwell has attributed similar misgivings to him:

The real problem of the West, as he saw it, was to preserve mankind's ethical values—honor, mercy, justice, respect for others—in the face of an almost universal disappearance of a belief in the immortality of the soul. Being naturally a good man, he was a good humanist, but being a logical man, he saw that others were not. When people ceased to be Christians, they did not necessarily become good humanists but superstitious fanatics and political madmen.[5]

It seems safe to assume that the process of de-Christianization and secularization, which has gone on so long, will not soon be reversed. It will continue, with consequences that will more and more obviously affect the whole tone and even the structure of our society. One of them—a minor one, no doubt, in the eyes of many, but pertinent to the subject of this paper—will be to make the position of Catholics (and members of other churches) one of greater isolation and alienation from the rest of the community. Peter L. Berger some years ago went so far as to say: "By the 21st century, religious believers are likely to be found only in small sects, huddled together to resist a worldwide secular culture."[6] His view may be too bleak and probably is, but we are moving in the direction he suggests.

De-Christianization could have taken many forms—that of an aggressive atheism, for example, as in the Soviet Union. In the West, however, it has run parallel with and has to a large extent been identified with liberalism. Liberalism undeniably has certain accomplishments to its credit; respect for the dignity of the individual is the greater because of it. But the individualism which is the essence of liberalism, and which is expressed in its twin ideals of liberty and equality, has had a corrosive effect on our culture.

To put it briefly, liberalism has made freedom the essential and defining characteristic of man. Man is by nature the free animal, and his basic natural good is freedom. In order to safeguard this central value, liberals have often opted for agnosticism in religion, skepticism in philosophy, and relativism in morals—and understandably so. If the chief good is individual freedom, then all other goods must be judged in relation to it. Truth itself—whether religious, philosophical, or moral— must be subordinated to the requirements of the individual's liberty.

Any assertion of an objective and transcendent truth thus becomes a threat to freedom. The one conviction on which free men can agree is that orthodoxy is dangerous. Hence, as the late John Courtney Murray, S.J., once remarked, modern man has "a horror of the absolute."

But it is this horror of the absolute that lies at the root of the sense of meaninglessness and purposelessness that pervades so much of modern literature and of life as people actually live it. It is also the explanation of the growing loss of ability to found community on any commonly held set of beliefs. At a deeper level it is the reason why an increasing number of people reject even the idea that community need be founded on common beliefs.

As Philip Rieff pointed out in his *The Triumph of the Therapeutic*,[7] cultures historically have had the function of enabling individuals to transcend themselves and their private desires by accepting communal beliefs, ideals, norms, and rituals. "Culture," he said, "is another name for a design of motives directing the self outward, toward those communal purposes in which alone the self can be realized and satisfied." But now we are asking "the question whether our culture can be so reconstructed that faith—some compelling symbolic of self-integrating communal purpose—need no longer superintend the organization of personality." A new symbolic, he felt, is emerging, which he described as "a doctrine developed for the private wants of private men."[8]

The visible manifestation of the process is the growing number of groups seeking "liberation" from socially established moral norms. They are particularly active in the revolt against traditional sexual morality, but in other areas as well. Always their claim is that the imposition of a social norm of conduct is a violation of the fundamental equality of men (if one may be pardoned for including women as well in that term), which is an equality in individual freedom.

One may imagine, as John Stuart Mill did in his essay, *On Liberty*, that the release of individual preferences from social control would lead to a richer, more variegated, and progressive society. Mill's argument for liberty was premised on the assumption that through open discussion and experimentation with different styles of living, men would come to know which ways of life were better and would choose them. As mankind progressed under a regime of freedom, he believed, opinions would converge upon more elevated standards of manner and morals. But the liberalization of society since Mill's day seems to have produced a somewhat different result. The old consensus on manners and morals has disintegrated at an accelerating pace, and cultural norms have been leveled down rather than up. The emancipation of the individual and the privatization of moral standards have brought about a general lowering and flattening out of norms. Far from moving to higher levels, we are inclined today to deny that there is any valid hierarchy of values by which higher and lower could be distinguished.

It is not, however, that the liberal society has abandoned all morality. It has, rather, gradually shifted and will continue to shift from an ethic based on the doctrines of revealed religion and natural law to a new ethic that makes fewer and less exacting demands on the individual, and aims only at goals that contribute to the pursuit of personal happiness in this world. This new ethic is a compound of humanitarianism and utilitarianism.

The new ethic may seem to be merely a secularized version of Christian charity, and in its origins it undoubtedly was. There is surely nothing anti-Christian in the desire to relieve suffering and to promote happiness. But as we have moved farther out of the Christian past and its inherited moral assumptions, we have conceived our humanitarian aims in more and more secular terms, and have more and more relativized our moral judgments on the permissible means of achieving them. Thus it is that we have come, in Fitzjames Stephen's words, to "reconsider the law of murder, and especially the law of infanticide." Nor are we finished yet. The legal-moral issues of the next quarter of a century will arise out of our growing utilitarianism about the means of pursuing our secular ends. Then we shall discover how far a post-Christian population can go in its search for satisfaction and its flight from pain.

The new morality, humanitarian in its goals and utilitarian in its judgment on means, is the prevailing ethic of contemporary liberal societies. It represents not merely the release of previously enforced controls on individual conduct, but the emergence of a new set of social norms. It is no accident, for instance, that the idealism of youth today is seldom directed toward self-conquest and self-discipline—these are easily dismissed as "masochism"—but almost always toward social justice and the reform of institutions.

These ideals, when analyzed, turn out to consist in the liberation of mankind from poverty, disease, psychic deprivations of various kinds, and social inequalities that are not clearly justified by service to other persons. The humanitarian-utilitarian ethic regards suffering as the absolute evil and individual self-fulfillment as the highest good, and elaborates its social goals accordingly. Egoism is sublimated into altruism when men come to understand that the price of seeking their own happiness is to help others to do the same.

Modern society, therefore, however rooted its ethic may be in enlightened self-interest, does have its preferred social goals, and these breed social norms. Being tolerant, society may with an even hand guarantee people the right to hold a religious faith, to have children and educate them in that faith, and to endure suffering unto death or, conversely, to hold no faith, to prevent the conception of children, to abort them when conceived, and to choose "death with dignity" rather than endure suffering. Nonetheless, no society, however tolerant, is or can be really neutral.

The values of the majority or of the dominant forces in the community determine the norms that society will favor or even impose, by the pressure of public opinion if not by the force of law. The attitudes which the press and the other media of communication foster, the content of public education, the policies of social welfare agencies, and the structure of the tax laws are only some of the ways in which the prevailing social norms manifest themselves.

These norms predictably will become more secular and post-Christian as we move toward the twenty-first century. Churches that want to remain alive and in contact with their people will be tempted to adopt the new norms, relying on theologians to find the language in which to present them as modernized versions of the Christian ethic. It is hard, after all, to swim against the mainstream.

But swimming with it also involves risks. People may notice the incompatibility of the humanitarian-utilitarian ethic with certain features of the gospel. Or they may simply conclude that a church that tells them only what the post-Christian society tells them has become irrelevant. The effort to check the decline of religious faith by adaptation to the secular culture is likely to be self-frustrating.

Public opinion polls may not furnish a very reliable insight into the inner life of a church. But what light they throw indicates that in the decade following Vatican II, a large percentage of the members of the Catholic Church in America have accepted the prevailing ethic in regard to artificial contraception, premarital sexual intercourse, remarriage after divorce, and legalization of abortion. At the same time their respect for the clergy has gone down, and they are more inclined than formerly to reject the authority of the Pope and bishops in matters of faith and morals. Their attendance at weekly Mass and the frequency of their confession of sins have also dropped. One may hail these developments as an emancipation of the masses from ecclesiastical tyranny. But they are hardly a sign of the growing spiritual vitality of the American Catholic Church. Nor do they suggest that the future of the Church in the United States lies with those Catholics who most fully conform to the surrounding culture.

Those churches that resist the tide, on the other hand, will be faced with the decline of American pluralism. It is not to be expected that our society, as it evolves, will continue to foster a greater variety of cultural and religious institutions. It will give wider scope to vagaries of individual conduct. But the institutions that both reflect and shape a culture—the schools and universities, the media of communication, the agencies of social welfare, for example—will be more and more cast in the secularist mold. It may appear to be self-contradictory to assert that as people lose their ability to found the community on definite and strongly held beliefs, their culture will become more homogenized. But it really is not; the two processes reinforce rather than oppose each other.

In an increasingly industrialized and interdependent society, the role of government will become greater, not less. It is more and more accepted today that it is ultimately the responsibility of government to keep the economy functioning at a satisfactory level, to provide at least a minimal standard of material well-being for the entire population, to furnish an education for all, to promote the social and economic advancement of groups that have suffered from discrimination, to protect the physical environment, to foster public health, and, finally, to control the growth of population. Where government does not pursue these goals through public institutions, it seeks to direct private institutions toward them by legal regulation and by the expenditure of public money. Since private, nonprofit educational and other welfare agencies have generally become dependent on public funds, they are under considerable pressure to conform. We must expect this trend to continue and to grow.

Society will not greatly care whether the individual believes in Christianity, Buddhism, atheism, or pederasty. But its government, as well as the great concentrations of corporate and other private wealth, will have practical tasks to perform in order to keep society going. However sharp the political disagreements concerning those tasks, they will be defined in general terms by the prevailing humanitarian-utilitarian ethic.

Society will therefore throw the weight of opinion, influence, and money against institutions that deviate from the prevailing ethic, particularly if they become obstacles to the execution of policies based on that ethic. Conversely, it will support and favor institutions that pursue socially approved goals. To reverse the gospel saying, where the public's heart is, there also will it put its treasure.

The result will be a regime in which the individual may believe what he pleases and do what he wants, so long as it does not clearly and directly harm others. And he may join with others to organize any kind of institution he wishes. But, unless the founders of the institution are able to support it with the private resources of a limited group and are content to operate on the fringes of society, it had better be built on the liberal and secular model. That is the only kind of institution that the secular state or the great corporations and foundations will endow. On the other hand, in a culture largely drained of faith, the number and size of groups willing and able to support a vigorous, well-developed institutional life of their own will diminish. The post-Christian society will be less, not more, pluralistic than the America of the nineteenth and early twentieth centuries.

Certain decisions of the U.S. Supreme Court in the past three decades, which have earlier been discussed, have also helped to push the country toward an homogenized secular culture. The Court has cut off virtually all substantial public aid to church-related elementary and secondary schools. At the same time it has insisted on the secularization of the public schools. In an effort to make all beliefs equal before the law, the Court has also subjectivized the legal definition of religion by making it identical with the content of the individual conscience, whatever that content may be. In addition, the Court has created a constitutional "right of privacy" that effectively removes important areas of conduct from legal regulation. It was on this ground that laws on contraception and abortion were found unconstitutional, and the Court now has in its hands the means by which it can purge from our laws whatever remnants of the earlier consensus on law and morals it chooses.

In this situation one must anticipate a decline in the institutional life of the American Catholic community. In the field of education the decline is already manifest. The *New York Times* reported at the end of 1974:

> The size of the Catholic school system has steadily shrunk. According to figures of the National Conference of Catholic Bishops, there were 13,360 high schools and elementary schools in 1964 with a combined enrollment of 5,625,040. Ten years later the number of schools had dropped to 10,349 with a registration of 3,629,646.[9]

The shrinkage of the Catholic school system will doubtless continue, though probably not to the point where it will disappear altogether. Although Catholic colleges and universities are not so thoroughly cut off from public aid as the lower schools, their prospects are no brighter than those of private higher education generally. Warnings abound today that a sizeable number of private colleges and universities will not survive the next ten or fifteen years. The Catholic ones among them, not well endowed financially and deprived by the dwindling number of religious vocations of the low-cost services of the religious orders on which they formerly depended, will be particularly hard hit.

To conclude, being Catholic in America will mean belonging to a Church that will have lost a large number of its institutions and a large part of its membership to the post-Christian secular society. It will mean maintaining a faith in the transcendent and eternal in a culture increasingly unable to appreciate it. It will mean being more sharply at odds with prevailing moral standards. It will mean continuing conflict with other groups in the population as the drive is pressed to remove from the law the moral values built into it during the Christian centuries.

So long as American society remains tolerant, Catholics will not become what they were accused of being under the Roman Empire, a *gens lucifuga,* a people who flee the light. But they will be forced back to a large extent on the family and the parish as the institutions for preserving and passing on the Catholic faith. They will have to accept a rather high rate of loss of faith among their young people as they succumb to the influence of the circumambient moral and cultural atmosphere. For those who remain, the Church will have to develop not a new religion, but a new pastoral theology to define in contemporary practical terms what it means to be a Catholic: what are the truths on which the Church thinks it most urgently necessary to insist, what one must believe in order to be a Catholic, what one must do in order to be a good one.

Yet those Catholics who persevere will offer a genuinely Christian alternative within the post-Christian society. They will thereby perform a much-needed role. For, as C. S. Lewis once wrote, "Did you ever meet, or hear of, anyone who was converted from scepticism to a 'liberal' or 'demythologized' Christianity? I think when unbelievers come in at all, they come in a good deal further."[10] The American Catholics of tomorrow may be confident that there will always be those outside the fold who will find the Christian alternative attractive. As the pall of secular despair deepens, Catholics may well find themselves in the position of a city built upon a mountaintop.

Notes

1. "Many Mansions," *American Historical Review* 69 (1964): 315.

2. Lester G. Crocker, "Presidential Address," in Louis T. Milic, ed., *The Modernity of the Eighteenth Century* (Cleveland: Case Western Reserve University Press, 1971), pp. xviii–xix.

3. "About Equality," *Commentary* 54 (1972): 42.

4. First published 1873; second edition of 1874 republished, ed. R. J. White (Cambridge: Cambridge University Press, 1967), 48.

5. *Time*, 15 November 1968, p. 110.

6. "A Bleak Outlook is Seen for Religion," *New York Times*, 25 February 1968, p. 3.

7. New York: Harper & Row, 1966.

8. Ibid., 4, 5, 50.

9. 29 December 1974, p. 12.

10. *Letters to Malcolm* (New York: Harcourt, Brace & World, 1963), 119.

9

Our Pluralistic Society

The American people, forming one political society, are politically one people. We rejoice in the unity established by the Constitution and symbolized by the flag. Yet we are also many peoples, with a large and multiplying diversity of beliefs, cultures, morals, manners, and lifestyles. We are urged to rejoice in our pluralism, too, and to see it as America's peculiar glory that she combines unity and diversity with a success not hitherto or elsewhere known: e pluribus unum. Our pluralism is held up to us, not merely as a fact to which we must perforce adjust our legal and political structures, but as a norm to which we should gladly conform. It is good to be pluralistic because it is precisely our pluralism that makes possible the highest of our values, liberty.

All societies, of course, are pluralistic to a greater or lesser extent; there is no such thing as a simply monolithic society. Not all societies, however, are free, and governments have frequently justified their suppression of freedom by the alleged necessity of preserving political unity against the centrifugal thrust of pluralism. The Spanish government under Generalísimo Franco, for example, would not let Catalans or Basques use their own language in public print or on the airwaves. The American genius has been to see how pluralism could be made the source of both unity and liberty.

James Madison gave classic expression to this view of pluralism in the most famous of the Federalist Papers, no. 10, during the campaign for the ratification of the newly proposed Constitution of the United States in 1787. First, he argued, the division of society into "factions" is inevitable, and the more inevitable the more developed a society is, for the causes of factions are "sown in the nature of man."

Communio (1982)

A zeal for different opinions concerning religion, concerning government, and many other points, as well of speculation as of practice; an attachment to different leaders ambitiously contending for pre-eminence and power; or to persons of other descriptions whose fortunes have been interesting to human passions, have, in turn, divided mankind into parties, inflamed them with mutual animosity, and rendered them much more disposed to vex and oppress each other than to cooperate for their common good. So strong is this propensity of mankind to fall into mutual animosities, that where no substantial occasion presents itself, the most frivolous and fanciful distinctions have been sufficient to kindle unfriendly passions and excite their most violent conflicts. But the most common and durable source of factions has been the various and unequal distribution of property. Those who hold and those who are creditors, and those who are debtors, fall under a like discrimination. A landed interest, a manufacturing interest, a mercantile interest, a moneyed interest, with many lesser interests, grow up of necessity in civilized nations, and divide them into different classes, actuated by different sentiments and views.[1]

Unavoidable though faction is, however, Madison recognized that it creates a danger for a people that intends to be free. A tyrannical government could tame the factions by depriving them of their freedom to organize and act politically. But it is otherwise under a freely elected republican form of government: "The regulation of these various and interfering interests forms the principal task of modern legislation and involves the spirit of party and faction in the necessary and ordinary operations of government."[2] The clashing interests must be reconciled and harmonized by the very people who form or who represent the interest groups.

The danger in a democratic republic was that those who had the most votes—the majority—would tyrannize over the minority without regard to private rights or the common welfare. Madison's remedy for this danger was ingenious. Ratify the Constitution, he urged, unite the states under the strong but limited government of an extensive republic, and you will find that, although the country will be governed by majority rule, the majorities will ordinarily be harmless. For, on the national scale, majorities will be shifting coalitions formed by persons of a variety of beliefs, interests, and ambitions. Such majorities are not likely to be tyrannical:

You make it less probable that a majority of the whole will have a common motive to invade the rights of other citizens; or if such a common motive exists, it will be more difficult for all who feel it to discover their own strength, and to act in unison with each other. . . . A religious sect may degenerate into a political faction in a part of the Confederacy [i.e., the Union]; but the variety of sects dispersed over the entire face of it must secure the national council against any danger from that source. A rage for paper money, for an abolition of debts, for an equal division of property, or for any other improper or wicked project, will be less apt to pervade the whole body of the Union than a particular member of it.[3]

We can afford to be one people precisely because we are so thoroughly divided that it is unlikely that a factional majority, "actuated by some impulse of passion, or of interest, adverse to the rights of other citizens, or to the permanent and aggregate interest of the community,"[4] will gain control of our national government. Thus pluralism, far from being a threat to unity, becomes its strongest support *if the pluralism is sufficiently pronounced.* Religious freedom depends on the multiplicity of sects and political freedom on the variety of economic and other interests.

Madison quietly assumes, however, that the pluralism will not be too pronounced. Prone though men are to use power unjustly, well though we "know that neither moral nor religious motives can be relied on as an adequate control" on this propensity,[5] Madison nonetheless takes it for granted that, at least on sober second thought, the bulk of the American people will agree that there are rationally discernible norms of justice, that people do have valid rights, and that some "projects" are "improper or wicked." Underlying the pluralism there is a *consensus juris*, an agreement about justice and right, sufficient to keep pluralism from tearing the nation apart.[6]

It is on this point that Madison has been criticized in one of the minor classics of twentieth-century American political theory, Robert A. Dahl's *A Preface to Democratic Theory.*[7] Professor Dahl is one of the most distinguished members of the school of political scientists known, if only to their critics, as "pluralists." Madison's argument rests, he says, on the idea of natural rights. That is its irremediable flaw because "the logic of natural rights seems to require a transcendental view in which the right is 'natural' because God directly or indirectly wills it," and "such an argument inevitably involves a variety of assumptions that at best are difficult and at worst impossible to prove to the satisfaction of anyone of positivist or skeptical predispositions."[8]

Dahl, therefore, shifts his own essentially Madisonian model of democratic government from the foundation of natural right and justice and bases it on the equality of all preferences. He proposes "to lay down political equality as an end to be maximized, that is, to postulate that the goals of every adult citizen of a republic are to be accorded equal value in determining governmental policies."[9] Madison relied on pluralism to prevent the tyranny of the majority and did not think he was talking nonsense, because to him the term, tyranny, was meaningful as a violation of natural rights. Dahl, since he finds natural rights (or any principle of natural justice) highly dubious, lays down a postulate. The goals of every adult citizen are to be accorded equal value, not because they have any value at all that reason could discern, but because, in the absence of any rational standard for comparing values, we stipulate that all goals are equal. The *consensus juris* is replaced by a formal agreement to treat all adult citizens' values as equal. Justice thus loses all substantive content and becomes pure form.

The views of a single political scientist may not in themselves be of great significance. But Dahl gives scholarly expression to what is now the dominant view in articulate public opinion. We are now to be protected, in this view, not from tyranny, but from the imposition of anyone's or any group's values on anyone else. No opinion and no policy can be regarded as legitimate which threatens to conflict with this supreme norm of "our pluralistic society." It is a society uncommitted, not only to any particular religious beliefs, but also to any particular moral principles. That means, however, that it is independent of all moral principles because, if all moral beliefs are subjective, then all principles embodied in them are inherently particular. The pluralistic society, therefore, stands upon no moral principles but is unified only by the procedural principle of an official neutrality that treats all beliefs equally.

I have argued earlier that in a society so conceived and so dedicated, the pluralist game becomes a confidence game by which certain groups press government into the service of their beliefs and goals under the pretense of preserving neutrality among all beliefs. There is no need to repeat that argument here, but I will illustrate it by citing an article by another author.

The U.S. Supreme Court in *Roe v. Wade*[10] made a woman's freedom to decide on an abortion a constitutional right and thereby committed the nation to an official neutrality concerning the life or death of an unborn child. As Steven R. Valentine points out, however, one result of that "neutrality" is that there are now more than sixty published decisions of courts awarding recovery of damages for "wrongful birth," i.e., for the failure of a doctor to provide parents with information about possible defects in their unborn child that would have led them to get an abortion. The proliferation of such decisions, plus the predictable improvement of means of diagnosing defects while a child is still in the womb, says Valentine, "will have the inescapable result of placing the physician under a legal duty to perform, or at least to recommend or suggest, some type of prenatal diagnostic test for 'defects' during every pregnancy—that, in short, no doctor who values his economic security will be able to afford not to prescribe such evaluations."[11] The alleged neutrality of the state toward abortion thus has the consequence of forcing doctors into an active cooperation with abortion, whatever their own moral convictions. This kind of result must follow in a multitude of other areas of life in which the very effort of the state to be neutral toward all beliefs puts the power of the state into the service of some beliefs as against others—and that is why the pluralist game, as currently played, is a shell game.

There is another reason why mere public neutrality cannot be an adequate rule for the government of a pluralistic society. As Thomas A. Spragens, Jr., has said in a recent and excellent book, a theory of the pluralistic society based on the subjectivity and relativity of all values undermines the society that it purports to justify and support:

> The pluralist model may impute more stability to contemporary secular democracy than it in fact possesses. Once he has interpreted American democracy as an embodiment of interest-group liberalism, the pluralist takes note of the relative continuity and stability of American democracy and concludes by imputing stability to interest-group liberalism. In fact, it may well be that, the more fully the American polity approximates the pattern of interest-group liberalism, the more unstable it may become. To the extent that the policies of such a system are increasingly perceived as the product of purely self-interested logrolling, the more that system will be subjected to intensified demands and afflicted by loss of support. The system loses support because it loses its moral legitimacy, and intensified demands are placed on it as each group seeks to compensate for the real or imagined influence of its rivals. For both reasons, the system suffers from an erosion of its authority and, with it, a diminution of its capacity to govern effectively. The system thus becomes progressively less stable.[12]

We may grant the measure of truth in Madison's contention that a plurality of religious sects and economic interests helps to prevent domination by any one of them over the rest. But if the pluralist game has no higher purpose than to prevent the imposition of some people's values on others, it loses credibility as an honest game and erodes the authority of the state.

The question of how the pluralist game might be played more honestly and effectively is important, unavoidable, and unanswerable in the abstract. There is no begging the question because there is no denying that we do live in a pluralistic society. We should indeed do well to demythologize pluralism and cease regarding it as an ideal. But it is a social fact with which we must deal. The question of how to deal with it, however, no longer admits of being answered by the clear and simple abstractions of liberal egalitarianism. There is no universally applicable blueprint for the government of a pluralistic society.

We must, therefore, learn to doubt the liberal assumption that the basic questions of political theory can be reduced to determining the proper relationship between the state and the individual. The assumption is an old one with roots reaching back into the Middle Ages. As the German scholar Otto Gierke said, it was medieval political theory that forged the weapons with which modern political theory fought its battles: "A combat it was in which the Sovereign State and the Sovereign Individual contended over the delineation of the provinces assigned to them by Natural Law, and in the course of that struggle all intermediate groups were first degraded into the position of the more or less arbitrarily fashioned creatures of mere Positive Law, and in the end were obliterated."[13]

Theologian Stanley Hauerwas has pointed out how the process described by Gierke has shaped the American idea of freedom in society:

> The state is understood only as one important actor in society; it does not replace the role or authority of other institutions such as the church, education or the family. This form of government is insured by basic rights guaranteed by law, such as assembly, speech, elections and assured transfer of power. Thus, democracies respect not only the rights of individuals but of other institutions which are necessary to keep the state limited. In effect, the rights of the individual have become the secular equivalent to the church as the means to keep government in its proper sphere.

But, says Hauerwas, this way of keeping government limited is deceptive because it leads us to ignore the

> fundamental tension between our commitments to the rights of the individual, preservation of intermediate associations, and the ability to retain a limited state. Indeed, the very language of "intermediate associations" already betrays liberal presuppositions which distort the moral reality of such institutions as the family. Whatever else the family is, it is not but another voluntary association. The very means used to insure that the democratic state be a limited state—namely, the rights of the individual—turn

out to be no less destructive for intermediate institutions than the monistic state of Marxism. For it is the strategy of liberalism to insure the existence of the "automony of cultural and economic life" by insuring the freedom of the individual. Ironically, that strategy results in the undermining of intermediate associations because they are now understood only as those arbitrary institutions sustained by the private desires of individuals.[14]

We must now get over the centuries-old habit of thinking of politics in terms of the sovereign state and the sovereign individual, and learn to think of a pluralistic society as a community of communities, not merely of individuals. We must also abandon the notion that in a pluralistic society the state can and should be neutral on all matters of morality about which there is disagreement among the people, lest the values of some be imposed on others. This notion leads to the establishment of the beliefs of the most secularized, materialistic, and hedonistic elements of the population as normative. If we are a plurality of communities, then the ability of the constituent communities to maintain and transmit their beliefs and values is at least as important as the freedom of the individual to live as he pleases.

We must therefore accept the fact that a free and pluralistic society exists, not by adherence to the rules of liberal individualism, but by an unending series of accommodations among its constituent communities; and we must allow political leaders to make the accommodations. These will vary from one pluralistic society to another. There is, in fact, no single, universally valid model of "the" pluralistic society. There are only pluralistic societies living, at best, under such arrangements as can win the support of the bulk of the citizens. The necessity of accommodation among communities is obvious in sharply divided societies such as Lebanon (which managed fairly well until the entrance of the Palestinians), Canada (which still functions fairly well but could cease to do so), and Northern Ireland (which has never worked well because of the unwillingness of the majority to make accommodations). Communal accommodation is less obviously but nonetheless necessary in other pluralistic societies such as America where, as Madison hoped, the divisions among the people are politically less explosive because there are so many of them. Even here we are dealing, not merely with individuals, all of whom are equal in their abstract individuality, but with the members of a variety of communities. A large part of the task of politics in our pluralistic society consists in accommodating the interests of these communities to one another.

The pluralist political scientists might not disagree with the discussion so far because it appears to correspond to their conception of interest-group liberalism. As Robert Dahl puts it, in our political system, "the making of governmental decisions is not a majestic march of great majorities united upon certain matters of basic policy. It is the steady appeasement of relatively small groups."[15] It goes without saying that any group that is willing to organize itself and acquire some political "clout" may play the game and get itself appeased.

Interest-group liberalism is surely a more realistic description of the American political process than what we may call "American Civil Liberties Union liberalism," with its narrow vision of individuals versus the state. But interest-group liberalism springs from the same root and suffers from the same fundamental flaw as ACLU liberalism. Group interests, that is to say, are regarded only as individual preferences written large and organized for action in the political arena.

As Spragens pointed out, interest-group liberalism erodes the moral legitimacy and authority of the political society. We may add that it regards with indifference the substantive nature of the lesser communities that constitute the pluralist society. Any group, united around any interest, is an interest group, and all that we may demand of it is that it be willing to play the pluralist game according to the rules.

A viable pluralist society, however, depends on more than agreement on the formal rules of the game. In the accommodations that it makes among its constituent communities, it trades constantly on consensus.[16] The accommodations work because of the substantive moral, cultural, and political convictions which people still share and which underlie and contain their disagreements. Different communities can live together as constituent parts of a larger national society only to the extent that they are held together by more than merely legal and material bonds. Otherwise they split apart, like Greeks and Turks on Cyprus, or live uneasily together in a relationship characterized by arrogance and fear on one side and festering resentment on the other. To this situation no set of merely formal rules of liberal democracy or bills of individual rights can be adequate.

Acceptance of the need for constant accommodation among communities leads to the conclusion, already noted above, that the question of how to play the pluralist game is not answerable in the abstract. The concrete answers that prove to be workable will vary from one pluralistic society to another and, within the same society, will vary from one period of time to another. The arrangements arrived at, therefore, are worked out by the judgments of political prudence, not by those of an abstract rationalism.

As Edmund Burke said well, "The rules and definitions of prudence can rarely be exact; never universal."[17] "For you know," as he explained in another place, "that the decisions of prudence (contrary to the system of the insane reasoners) differ from those of judicature; and that almost all the former are determined on the more or the less, the earlier or the later, and on a balance of advantage and inconvenience, of good and evil."[18]

There is, for example, no universal answer to the question, If a pluralistic society is made up of communities, what will rank as a community? Canada is officially bilingual because it contains two distinct linguistic communities. The United States recognizes only English as an official language, and there is considerable controversy over the wisdom of the concessions we have made to bilingualism in education. Yet, if Puerto Rico were to join the Union as a state, some accommodation to official bilingualism would have to be made. Whether linguistic communities are to be recognized depends very much on circumstances.

Furthermore, while we may admit that, depending on circumstances, recognition and some degree of accommodation to linguistic, cultural, ethnic, or racial communities may be wise and just, are we to accord the same to every group that presents itself as a "community"? Should we, for example, take masochists, fetishists, and homosexuals as forming communities? The late Justice William Douglas of the U.S. Supreme Court did so when he claimed constitutional protection for publications that were "of value to the masochistic community or to others of the deviant community."[19] Justice Douglas was admittedly a droll fellow and not to be taken seriously, but he was only using the standard rhetoric of liberal pluralism: any group that has anything in common is a community and should be treated as equal to other communities.

If we are unwilling to make the slide into sheer subjectivism implied in that proposition, then we must agree on some criteria by which to judge which groups will be accepted as communities. That entails deciding which communal values are genuinely human ones that deserve recognition. That in turn assumes that there exists, even in our pluralist society, what the Middle Ages called the *major et sanior pars*, a larger and sounder part of society that is capable of making the decision. In order to make this last assumption, it is helpful and probably necessary to agree that human reason can arrive at some grasp of moral truths, and that through rational discussion human beings can reach rational moral conclusions.

There is also no abstract and universally applicable answer to the question of how pluralistic a society can be and still remain a single society. Modern liberalism has favored maximizing individual liberty in order to reconcile unity with diversity. A society populated by liberal individuals will contain social groups, of course, but the groups will be numerous, not very large in size, and rather fluid in membership. People will tend to move in and out of these groups freely, and so they will not threaten the unity and stability of the liberal pluralistic society. Strong, cohesive, and lasting communities within the society, however, are feared as a threat to unity: they are, as we say, divisive. Liberalism, therefore, in its own way frowns on diversity and tries to discourage it. Wear any style of clothes you want, it tells us, or none at all, but do not believe deeply in anything that might introduce a divisive issue into politics.

There is undeniably ample evidence that the division of a society into a small number of strong and cohesive communities can tear the society apart. But if we carry liberal individualism to its logical term in order to preserve unity through pluralism, we shall learn that this solution, too, carries a price. The constant disparagement of particular communities and their beliefs, and the steady subordination of their cherished ideals to the unity and stability of the political society end by robbing the political society itself of vitality and drying up the springs of political loyalty and love of country. Those who do not love their families, their kinsmen, their "own kind," their neighborhoods, or their churches are not likely to love a merely political unit or the democratic system. Edmund Burke again puts it well: "To be attached to the subdivision, to love the little platoon we belong to in society, is the first principle (the germ as it were) of public affections. It is the first link in the series by which we proceed toward a love to our country and to mankind."[20]

It is the particular communities within society that engender, nourish, and transmit the beliefs, affections, and loyalties that form the moral consensus on which society lives. Communities that radically dissent from the consensus do not perform this function, of course. But without communities which have strong bonds of belief and affection, there will be no soil out of which the consensus may grow. Without them, society may indeed be pluralistic in the sense of being made up of rootless individuals. But such people will not regard society and its political system as anything more than a utilitarian convenience.

Faith communities—which we ordinarily call churches—in particular must insist upon their distinctive beliefs if they are to perform their role in society. For, by an apparent paradox, the common elements of our religious tradition will be preserved and handed on only by those groups that take seriously the particular forms in which that tradition has come down to them. Christianity, which is the most widely held religion in this country, will for any foreseeable future not exist in a single denominational form. The Christian tradition is strongest among the denominations with the greatest attachment to their own beliefs and weakest among the denominations that are most ready to give up the beliefs that distinguish them from other denominations.

The divisions among Christians are deplorable, to be sure, but the remedy proposed for them by liberal Christians and overeager ecumenists is to pretend that the divisions are merely verbal or at least unimportant. The result is a shriveling of religious belief into a set of enlightened and progressive views. Conservative Protestants and orthodox Catholics, on the other hand, while firmly agreeing to disagree on points which they recognize as important, find areas in which they can cooperate to uphold the religious and moral convictions that they share. In some of these areas devout believing Jews are willing to join them.

Although the question of how to govern a pluralistic society is unanswerable in abstract and universal terms, certain suggestions can be made. The first is to refuse resolutely to accept the liberal definition of the question in terms of the individual and the state alone. Society is made up of communities on whose moral health society depends. Pluralism does not require that the communities and their moral beliefs be sacrificed to the equality of all individual preferences. The larger and sounder part of society must have the right and the power to determine the moral limits of permissible action. If the larger part is in fact not the sounder part of society, then society will certainly be in peril—but it will not escape the danger by resorting to an unrestrained liberal individualism.

To be more specific, public policy may and ought to take the monogamous family as the basic unit of society, and should support and encourage it in its culture-transmitting function. To aid the family in this function, and to support the different religious and cultural communities to which families belong, the educational system ought to become more open and flexible than it now is. We need to rethink the notion that the secularized public school is the rock on which the republic stands. It may have been possible so to conceive of the public school when it was the agent of a dominant Anglo-Saxon Protestant culture. But now Protestants who are concerned to maintain what is left of that culture would do well to think of other and better relationships among the state, the communities, and the schools.

Finally, while it is not and should not be the function of the state to teach religion, it is in the interest of the society that the state governs that religion should be taught. We need consequently to rethink the proposition that religious freedom consists primarily or exclusively in a separation of church and state made as absolute as possible. Political society and the state depend on social forces that they cannot create but can destroy, and among these religion is one of the principal ones. Some relationship between the state and religion more nuanced than neutrality between religion and irreligion is needed, in the interest of society and the state.

These are suggestions that will go down hard, if they go down at all in the present climate of American public opinion. The alternative, however, is a steady degeneration of pluralism into mere individualism. That is a prospect that even liberals, if they are intelligent, may contemplate with some dismay.

Notes

1. Alexander Hamilton, John Jay, and James Madison, *The Federalist* (New York: Modern Library, n.d.), 55–56.

2. Ibid., 56.

3. Ibid., 61–62.

4. Ibid., 54.

5. Ibid., 58.

6. Ibid., 365.

7. Chicago: University of Chicago Press, 1956.

8. Ibid., 45.

9. Ibid., 32.

10. 410 U.S. 113 (1973).

11. "When the Law Calls Life Wrong," *Human Life Review* 8 (1982): 46, 47, and 53, n. 3.

12. *The Irony of Liberal Reason* (Chicago: University of Chicago Press, 1981), 303.

13. *Political Theories of the Middle Age*, trans. Frederick William Maitland (1900, reprinted Boston: Beacon Press, 1958), 100.

14. "Symposium," *Center Journal* 1, 3 (1982): 44–45.

15. *Preface to Democratic Theory*, 146.

16. In fairness to Professor Dahl, it should be noted that he is well aware of this. See ibid., 132–33.

17. *First Letter on a Regicide Peace*, in *The Works of the Right Honourable Edmund Burke*, 16 vols. (London: Rivington, 1803–1827) 8:87.

18. *Letter to Sir Hercules Langrishe* in *Works* 6:309.

19. Dissenting opinion, *Ginzburg v. U.S.*, 383 U.S. 463, 489 (1966).

20. *Reflections on the Revolution in France*, in *Works* 5:100.

10

Unity in Diversity

A colleague once assured me that the only bond of unity holding the American people together was an agreement on procedures. We agree to settle disputes that arise among us by following constitutionally and legally defined procedures and to abide by the results. That is democracy as we understand it, and we need no other unity than agreement on the procedures of democracy.

That agreement may be, in fact, the only unity we can have as our cultural and moral pluralism spreads and grows deeper. A people who increasingly disagree on basic moral principles may be able to agree only on procedures. Whether people will continue indefinitely to accept the outcome of the procedures in the absence of common moral principles, however, remains to be seen.

Carried far enough, pluralism can lead to that blend of libertarianism and egalitarianism that the liberal wing of the U.S. Supreme Court sees as the true meaning of the Constitution. According to these members, the freedom of the individual is our highest national value, but it is a freedom that must be guaranteed to all equally, without distinction of race, religion, morals, sex, or sexual preference. There may be and sometimes are social interests of a utilitarian nature (''compelling state interests'') that override individual freedom in particular cases, but they are never moral interests.

A recent clear example of this belief is the dissenting opinion that Justice Harry A. Blackmun wrote for all four dissenters in the 1986 case of *Bowers v. Hardwick*.[1] In that case a 5–4 majority of the Court upheld the constitutionality of a Georgia law that made sodomy a crime. Blackmun and his fellow dissenters protested that the Court should have

The World & I (September 1987)

struck the law down as unconstitutional. In their view, that the majority of people for centuries and even thousands of years had condemned homosexual relations as immoral was irrelevant. What mattered was that sodomy was an intimate personal relationship and, in the words of Justice Blackmun, "depriving individuals of the right to choose for themselves how to conduct their intimate relationships poses a far greater threat to the values most deeply rooted in our Nation's history than tolerance of nonconformity could ever do."[2]

Justice Byron White, on the other hand, speaking for the majority of the Court, replied that "to claim that a right to engage in such conduct is 'deeply rooted in this Nation's history and tradition' . . . is at best facetious." Furthermore, he said, no law is unconstitutional merely because it legislates morality. "The law is constantly based on notions of morality, and if all laws representing essentially moral choices are to be invalidated under the Due Process Clause [of the Fourteenth Amendment], the courts will be very busy indeed."[3]

The underlying issue in this case and a host of others is whether the Constitution allows the political community to have a public morality supported by law. Libertarian-egalitarians say no. Ronald Dworkin, professor of law at New York and Oxford Universities, speaks for many when he says that "political decisions must be, as far as possible, independent of any particular conception of the good life, or of what gives value to life. Since the citizens of a society differ in their conceptions, the government does not treat them as equals if it prefers one conception to another."[4] We are bound together, therefore, not by any shared idea of what constitutes a truly human life, but only by procedures designed above all to protect individual rights equally.

The opposing view is held by writers who are coming to be know as communitarians. According to them, community is as natural to man as individuality. We are obviously all individuals, but the human individual is by nature a social and political animal. It does no violence to his nature to live in community. On the contrary, he can realize his nature as a human being only by taking part in the life of a community.

But a community is not merely a mutual-protection association that individuals join for the sake of security in pursuing their essentially private goals. A community is constituted by shared beliefs and values. It is a community because it rejects certain conceptions of the good life (although it may tolerate them) and accepts others as the basis for its public moral judgments.

Both sides in this dispute will agree that the political community, or state, is not the only community, and that the ends of government are not coterminous with the ends of human life and human society. On any view that is compatible with our Constitution, human beings have individual and social goals that go beyond the legitimate goals of government. Constitutional government is limited government, and this means that not only are the powers of government limited but also that government serves limited purposes. The state is the highest community in its limited sphere, but it is not the only community and its purposes are not the only or the highest goals of human society.

Furthermore, when speaking of the Constitution of the United States, we must remember that it is the constitution of a federal system. It presupposes the existence of the constituent states of the union. These states draw their powers and their purposes, not from the Constitution, but from the distinct peoples of the respective states. The federal Constitution creates a more perfect union among the states by establishing a federal government. It confers on that government, not all the powers, but only certain powers that a constitutional government may have. The Tenth Amendment is not part of the original Constitution, but it only states explicitly what was implicit in the whole original Constitution: "The powers not delegated to the United States by the Constitution, nor prohibited by it to the States, are reserved to the States respectively, or to the people."

Our Constitution, therefore, is the legal framework of a political unity in diversity. Its preamble states in broad terms the purposes for which "we the people of the United States" established this framework: "to form a more perfect Union, establish Justice, insure domestic Tranquility, provide for the common Defense, promote the general Welfare and secure the Blessings of Liberty to ourselves and our Posterity." Broad as these terms are, however, they do not include all the ends that men historically have pursued through government (the propagation of religious truth, for example, is omitted).

The Constitution is our legal framework as a nation, but no mere legal document can create or maintain unity in diversity if the necessary social conditions for it are lacking. Cyprus, divided between Greek Christians and Moslem Turks; Lebanon, rent by multisided strife among Christians and Moslems and their subdivisions; and Northern Ireland, where the legitimacy of the state itself is a political issue, prove the point. Even such stable political systems as those of India, Canada, and Belgium illustrate the difficulty of uniting people sharply divided by religion and/or language. The constitution of a country can be a potent force in unifying it, but there is an antecedent unity upon which it must depend.

The authors of the *Federalist*, that first and classic commentary on our Constitution, were well aware of this truth. John Jay, who later became the first chief justice of the U.S. Supreme Court, argued in *Federalist 2* that America needed and was suited to "one federal government" because it already was one country both geographically and socially. America was "not composed of detached and distant territories" but was "one connected, fertile wide-spreading country," inhabited by "one united people—a people descended from the same ancestors, speaking the same language, professing the same religion, attached to the same principles of government, very similar in their manners and customs."[5] Jay's emphasis on the cultural unity that the American people already enjoyed may seem to have been contradicted by the later American experience of massive immigration from all over the world, but it points to a dimension of the problem of maintaining unity in diversity that we cannot ignore: Diversity cannot be so pronounced that it makes unity impossible.

Jay may also seem to be contradicted by his coauthor, James Madison, in the latter's famous *Federalist 10*. As we have seen, Madison's argument for ratifying the Constitution and thus establishing a large republic under a single national government was precisely that liberty depends on pluralism. Republican liberty, he said, inevitably breeds what he called factions and we call interest groups. In a republic, factions are dangerous to the rights of other groups and to the general interest of the community when they become large enough to form majorities, win elections, and impose their self-serving will upon minorities. The remedy, said Madison, is to make the republic so large that it will include so many factions that it is unlikely that any one of them can become a majority. Since we cannot avoid having factions if we mean to be free, the more factions—economic, political, and religious—the better. The very multiplicity of factions will prevent them from tyrannizing.

Madison had a view of human nature that we may call either jaundiced or realistic. People are selfish and we well know that "neither moral nor religious motives can be relied on as an adequate control" on their selfishness.[6] Nonetheless, he did not regard human nature as entirely depraved or deprived of a knowledge of elementary public morality. "Justice," he declared in *Federalist 51*, "is the end of government. It is the end of civil society. It ever has been and ever will be pursued until it be obtained, or until liberty be lost in the pursuit."[7] This passion for justice was the reason for Madison's confidence in the beneficent effect of multiplying factions:

> In the extended republic of the United States, and among the great variety
> of interests, parties, and sects which it embraces a coalition of a majority
> of the whole society could seldom take place on any other principles than
> those of justice and the general good.[8]

That proposition, however, makes no sense unless the American people, or at least the larger and sounder part of them, are capable of recognizing and accepting certain "principles of justice and the general
good." Madison relied heavily on certain mechanical structures to
maintain liberty: the division of sovereignty between the nation and the
states, the separation of powers and checks and balances in the national
government, and, above all, "the great variety of interests, parties, and
sects" that the extended republic would embrace. He thought that liberty needed these devices, which check the greed and ambition of some
by setting the greed and ambition of others against them, because neither religious nor moral motives were strong enough to make people
consistently control selfish passion. But neither did he think that a nation of radical skeptics or moral relativists would make the structures
work. Beneath the necessary pluralism there had to be a degree of moral
unity sufficient to make a workable agreement on justice and the general good possible.

In *Federalist 55*, Madison goes so far as to say that republican government depends more than other forms of government on the virtue of
its citizens:

> As there is a degree of depravity in mankind which requires a certain
> degree of circumspection and distrust, so there are other qualities in human
> nature which justify a certain portion of esteem and confidence. Republi-
> can government presupposes the existence of these qualities in a higher
> degree than any other form. Were the pictures which have been drawn by
> the political jealousy of some among us faithful likenesses of the human
> character the inference would be, that there is not sufficient virtue among
> men for self-government; and that nothing less than the chains of despo-
> tism can restrain them from destroying and devouring one another.[9]

It would be easy to multiply passages from other writers in the republican tradition, both European and American, who insist that democratic
republics cannot survive without citizens imbued with an adequate degree of civic virtue. If this be true, we must ask where the citizens
get the virtue necessary for civil liberty and self-government. Another
question may be asked: How do we determine what virtue is? Given
that individualism is so strong a strain in our national character, we find

this second question particularly difficult to answer. Yet the American people historically did answer these two questions more or less satisfactorily by drawing on a common tradition composed of the two strands of faith and reason.

A distinguished Catholic theologian once remarked that old-fashioned Protestantism was the bedrock on which the republic was founded and that Catholics should not rejoice at its disintegration. Protestantism has always been an individualistic religion founded on the principle of private judgment. The private believer was to judge, however, in accordance with a Scripture that all Christians held to be the inspired word of God. The arrival on these shores of masses of Catholics and Jews, although it diluted the nation's Protestantism, did not change substantial agreement on biblical morality. There were Ten Commandments, and all denominations of any numerical importance knew what they were.

There never was an Age of Innocence, of course, in which everyone lived by the Ten Commandments, but there was a time in this country's history when Americans generally acknowledged that they were God's commands and therefore the supreme standard of moral judgment. Our pluralistic society has traded on a widely shared religio-moral tradition. This tradition told citizens what virtue was and how to acquire it through prayerful obedience to God's law.

At this point many writers will rush to remind us that in the eighteenth century Deism was taken among the educated class to be "the religion of all sensible men," and that a good number of our Founding Fathers subscribed to it. Deism, or natural religion as it was often called, rejected biblical revelation as superstition, and held that unaided human reason could attain to all that men needed to know about God and their duties to Him. Although later history was to show that Deism was a halfway house to atheism, Deistic "natural morality" did not differ dramatically from biblical morality on matters of public concern and was in fact a secularized version of traditional Christian morality. The secularization eventually undermined the morality, but that consequence was not immediately obvious to most people.

Confidence in the ability of reason to arrive at moral truth was the companion strand (for Deists the only strand) to religious faith in the moral tradition. The political thought of the time also indicated an enormous confidence in reason. The men of the eighteenth century, and not only the Deists among them, regarded their century as uniquely the Age of Reason. Reason, as they understood it, supported their morals and dictated their liberal political theory.

Reason furnished the cement that held an individualistic and pluralistic society together. As previously indicated, the reason in which classical liberalism had such confidence traded upon a moral tradition of which revealed religion was the vehicle, if not the source. The current disintegration of this tradition is as much due to a loss of confidence in reason as to a decline of faith in divine revelation. Millions of Americans are no longer sure that either faith or reason can tell them what virtue is or how to acquire it. They are left with the uneasy feeling (or the passionate belief) that all individual opinions and appetites are morally equal and should be equal in the eyes of the law. Such currently topical issues as gay rights, surrogate motherhood, abortion, and euthanasia can hardly be resolved by reason in a nation in which "Whose reason?" is the first and final question because it is assumed that there are no objective moral truths that individuals can recognize and agree upon.

Yet a lack of moral consensus engenders certain risks for the future of democracy. If democratic politics comes to be seen as nothing more than a struggle among pressure groups, regulated by no common standards of justice, people will tend to lose faith in the democratic process. They will regard politics as a game in which winning is the only thing, nice guys finish last, and the good of the community is merely a slogan to deceive the gullible into making sacrifices for the unscrupulous. They may also come to feel that an unending assault on public standards of decency and morality, justified in the name of pluralism and tolerance, leaves them with little community and less common good to merit their devotion.

"Justice," as Madison said, "ever has been and ever will be pursued until it be obtained, or until liberty be lost in the pursuit." If he was right, it is essential that most citizens most of the time should believe that on the whole and in the long run democratic procedures produce just and good results. Faith in procedures, to that extent, therefore depends on faith in substantive standards of justice and virtue that transcend procedures.

We return, then, to the question: How do we as a political community determine what justice and virtue are? Historically, we have relied on a consensus derived from both faith and reason. It is not necessary to assert, and it is certainly not suggested here, that we ever made a formal national commitment to a particular religion or philosophy. All that is suggested is that as a matter of social fact we were able to carry on political debates and arrive at political decisions within a framework of commonly accepted moral principles. If we have lost that framework, as to a large extent we seem to have done, the question then is whether we can get it back again.

Insofar as a moral consensus depends on religion, it is the business of the churches, not of the political order, to restore it. The churches render a service to the political order by supplying moral underpinnings, but they will serve it all the better if they concentrate on teaching their faith for its own sake and not for the sake of its political consequences. For its part, the political order enables religion to perform its social role by guaranteeing the free exercise of religion, not by striving to drive religious influence out of public life by spinning out all possible implications of the phrase "an establishment of religion."

The role of reason in politics is more properly a political question, but again not one that can be answered by formal acts of government. We as citizens, however, may take a first step toward restoring confidence in reason by refusing to let skeptics and relativists beg the question with their a priori assumption that reason can tell us nothing about what is good for human beings. Human good is the ultimate object of and justification for politics, and we should not easily nor lightly admit that reason can lead us to no agreement on it.

More than thirty years ago, Walter Lippmann held up the ideal of a rational order of politics as the necessary condition of a viable democracy:

> The rational order consists of the terms which must be met in order to fulfill men's capacity for the good life in this world. They are the terms of the widest consensus of rational men in a plural society. They are the propositions to which all men concerned, if they are sincerely and lucidly rational, can be expected to converge.[10]

Lippmann was not widely listened to in the 1950s and the prospects for his being listened to today are even more bleak. On the other hand, if individual rights and civil liberties are used to keep rational minds from converging on the substantive principles of order, the prospects for unity in diversity may also be rather bleak.

Notes

1. 478 U.S. 186 (1986).
2. Ibid., 214.
3. Ibid., 194, 196.

4. "Liberalism," in Michael Sandel, ed., *Liberalism and Its Critics* (New York: New York University Press, 1984), 64.

5. Alexander Hamilton, John Jay, and James Madison, *The Federalist* (New York: Modern Library, n.d.), 8–9.

6. Ibid., 58.

7. Ibid., 340.

8. Ibid., 340–41.

9. Ibid., 365.

10. *The Public Philosophy* (New York: New American Library of World Literature/Mentor Books, 1955), 95.

11

Liberalism in Root and Flower

Pornography has become the hallmark of liberal democracy. When General Franco died and democracy returned to Spain, pornographic establishments blossomed all over Madrid, heralding the dawn of liberty. But the phenomenon was not a unique or peculiarly Spanish one. Throughout the democratic world pornography is the external sign of that bland, permissive tolerance that is now liberalism's sole remaining inward grace.

It may appear strange that liberal democrats should have come to accept mass pandering to a degraded taste as the symbol of their regime, but that they have done so is clear. Why they have done so, however, is a question that invites inquiry. The reason, upon inquiry, will turn out to have little to do with sex but much to do with the subjectivism that is the essence of liberalism.

John H. Hallowell described, over forty years ago, the original or "integral" liberalism of the seventeenth century in his *The Decline of Liberalism as an Ideology*.[1] It was based, he said, on a concept of individuality that emphasized "the inherent moral worth and spiritual equality of each individual, the dignity of human personality, the autonomy of individual will, and the essential rationality of men." Because of the importance attached to both autonomy and rationality, "two essential elements are found in liberalism in its integral form: first, the belief that society is composed of atomic, autonomous individuals; and, second, the belief that there are certain eternal truths transcending individuals and independent of either individual will or desire." Consequently, integral liberalism blended two different theories of law: "on the one hand, there is the notion that law is the product of individual

The Ethical Dimension of Political Life (1983)

115

wills and the embodiment of individual interests; on the other hand, there is the notion that law is the embodiment of eternal and absolute truths independent of either individual will or interest.''[2]

The foundation of integral liberalism, therefore, is a merging of ''the two concepts, despite their logical inconsistency and respective self-sufficiency, into one theory.'' The cement that held the two concepts together was conscience, conceived of as each individual's share of human reason. Integral liberalism, Hallowell explains,

> espoused freedom for the individual under the impersonal authority of law. It conceived of the law as being eternal, universal, and rational, and as containing substantive limitations upon subjective interest and will. To an anarchic conception of society as composed of autonomous individual units, liberalism opposed the conception of an order transcending individuals, and placed the responsibility for realizing this order, potentially embodied in eternal truths, upon individual reason and conscience. The link between the subjective will of the individual and the objective order was reason and conscience.[3]

The greater part of Hallowell's book is devoted to showing how the liberal synthesis fell apart under the impact of historicism and positivism. As people lost confidence in their ability, through reason, to know truths that transcend sense experience, reason became increasingly individualized and moral judgment turned into the mere expression of individual preference. The disintegration of the liberal synthesis paved the way in Germany, he argues, for the triumph of Hitlerism. But (as Hallowell, of course, is well aware) the liberal conception of reason contained within itself the seeds of this disintegration from the beginning. The subjective will of the individual eventually prevailed over the objective moral order because of the way in which liberals understood reason and its capacities.

Liberal rationalism has always contained a strong streak of hedonism. We may cite a few well-known English writers in the liberal tradition for illustration. The view of Thomas Hobbes as the author of that tradition is recent and admittedly controversial, but it is held by eminent scholars.[4] John Locke, too, is the subject of endless controversy, but Sheldon Wolin expresses a common opinion when he says, ''To the extent that modern liberalism can be said to be inspired by any one writer, Locke is undoubtedly the leading candidate.''[5] Jeremy Bentham brought into bold relief the utilitarianism that was implicit in liberalism. His somewhat recalcitrant disciple, John Stuart Mill, was the nineteenth-century liberal par excellence.

These writers began their moral reasoning by reducing "the good" to pleasure. Thus Hobbes: "Good, and evil are names that signify our appetites, and aversions. . . ."[6] Locke agrees:

> Things then are good or evil only in reference to pleasure or pain. That we call good, which is apt to cause or increase pleasure or diminish pain in us; or else to procure or preserve us the possession of any other good, or absence of any evil. And, on the contrary, we name that evil which is apt to produce or increase any pain or diminish any pleasure in us; or else to procure us any evil, or deprive us of any good.[7]

Bentham repeats the theme in these words: "Nature has placed mankind under the governance of two sovereign masters, pain and pleasure. It is for them alone to point out what we ought to do, as well as to determine what we shall do."[8] John Stuart Mill strove to free utilitarianism from the crudity of Bentham's quantitative analysis of pleasure and pain, and maintained in his *Utilitarianism* that pleasures differ in quality as well as in quantity. But he did not break with Bentham's thesis that pleasure and pain are the only springs of human action. He devoted chapter 4 of *Utilitarianism* to showing that "happiness is a good," that "there is in reality nothing desired except happiness," and that happiness is pleasure or the absence of pain, so that "to desire anything except in proportion as the idea of it is pleasant is a physical and metaphysical impossibility."[9]

It is important to notice at this point the effect that hedonism has upon rationalism. A philosophy that equates the good with pleasure severely limits the scope of reason. The whole realm of judgment on what is good or bad for human beings, therefore of normative ethical and political judgment, is closed to reason. This explains why Hobbes's laws of nature are only "conclusions, or theorems" of enlightened self-interest,[10] why Locke's efforts to set his law of nature on a firm rational foundation were unsuccessful,[11] and why Bentham declared that talk of natural rights was "simply nonsense . . . nonsense upon stilts."[12]

It also explains why Mill's *On Liberty*, although it is premised upon a theory of human development and progress, nonetheless insists on identifying development with the cultivation of individuality. For if the good is reducible to pleasure, and pleasure is a subjective and individual experience, then all judgments about the good must ultimately be felt preferences or aversions that are beyond the criticism of reason and intellect.

As we have seen, Robert Dahl concludes that, since the relative worth of different goals cannot be discerned by reason, the political system must postulate the equal worth of all adult citizens' desires. Thus political equality comes to be founded, by default, so to speak, on the subjectivity of all values. This is the direction in which the inner dynamism of liberal thought has moved it from the beginning. The substantive limitations upon subjective interest and will, which Hallowell pointed out in integral liberalism, broke down under the pressure of liberal hedonism.

Underlying the hedonism and subjectivism of the liberal mind is its individualism, and this in turn springs from its nominalism. Michael Oakeshott explains:

> Individualism as a gospel has drawn its inspiration from many sources, but as a reasoned theory of society it has its roots in the so-called nominalism of late medieval scholasticism, with its doctrines that the reality of a thing is its individuality, that which makes it this thing, and that in both God and man will is precedent to reason. Hobbes inherited this tradition of nominalism, and more than any other writer passed it on to the modern world. His civil philosophy is based, not on any vague belief in the value of sanctity of the individual man, but on a philosophy for which the world is composed of *individuae substantiae*.[13]

Locke's nominalism runs throughout his *Essay concerning Human Understanding*. The object of our knowledge, he holds, is our own ideas, and these are either sensations caused from without or our interior reflection on the operations of our own minds. From these elementary building blocks we compose the ideas that constitute our knowledge of the world. Consequently, we never know the real essence of a thing, but only its nominal essence, which is a mental construct that we make up for the sake of convenience in dealing with the world. Besides, the real essence of any substance, could we know it, would be its particular and individual constitution, that which makes it this thing and no other.[14] Locke's world, as much as Hobbes's, is a world of individual substances, known to us only in the sensations they cause in us.

Concerning Bentham, Crane Brinton remarks, "It may seem no small violence to Bentham's memory to describe him in a term drawn from the Middle Ages he so disliked, but he really is the perfect nominalist. The individual, John Doe, is for him an ultimate reality."[15] Mill's theory of knowledge is a more mixed bag, on the contents of which there are widely varying views among scholars. R. P. Anschutz, who has written an extended analysis of Mill's epistemology, sees him as oscillating between nominalism and realism, but coming down on the side of realism where science was concerned. "He was always a realist when he was in earnest about science: . . . and there are few philosophers who have been more thoroughly in earnest about science than Mill," says Anschutz. Mill could therefore hold a deterministic view of man in "the heavier treatises on scientific method like the *Logic*." But in "the more popular essays on ethics like the essay *On Liberty*," he could espouse "the romantic or self-formative view."[16] It is in his highly individualistic ethics that Mill's nominalism comes into play. The individual must decide upon his own good because it is so thoroughly his.

A few references to a few writers prove very little, of course. But one may venture the suggestion that the nominalist view of the world, which reduced it to a collection of individual substances only externally related to each other, furnishes a key to understanding what has happened to the liberal tradition. It explains, for one thing, why the idea of a moral law of nature, which still persisted in Hobbes and Locke (in however withered a form), was abandoned and replaced by scientific laws of nature of the sort that Bentham and Mill believed in.

For if, in our ignorance of the nature of anything, we cannot know its natural good, we may yet observe and apprehend the relations of efficient causality that obtain among things. And if, instructed by David Hume, we learn to doubt even our ability to know causality, we may yet perceive patterns among the data of the senses, patterns that can be expressed in statistical "laws" and may be explained by hypotheses that are at least conditionally valid. Our knowledge of the real, therefore, insofar as we have genuine knowledge, is simply knowledge of these aspects of reality that are quantifiable.

Such a view of the world has a tendency to make substances themselves disappear, because it depends on a particular method of analysis and synthesis. Just as we understand a clock when we can take it apart and put it together again, so we understand any other thing in particular and all things in general. As the Enlightenment *philosophe*, Jean le Rond d'Alembert, put it, "we can hope to know nature . . . by thoughtful study of phenomena, by the comparison we make among them, by the art of reducing, as much as that may be possible, a large number of phenomena to a single one that can be regarded as their principle."[17] The synthesis or reconstitution of the object analyzed shows how the subsidiary phenomena follow from the one or few basic phenomena, which are the principles from which the whole ensemble flows. This way of understanding things creates at least a temptation to regard the parts as more real than the whole because it is they that "explain" the whole: we understand something when we can reduce it, if only in thought, to its elements and see how they fit together again.

Michael Polanyi describes this view of scientific understanding in these words:

> The paradigm of a conception of science pursuing the ideal of absolute detachment by representing the world in terms of its exactly determined particulars was formulated by Laplace. An intelligence which knew at one moment of time—wrote Laplace—"all the forces by which nature is animated and the respective positions of the entities which compose it . . . would embrace in the same formula the movement of the largest bodies in the universe and those of the lightest atom: nothing would be uncertain for it, and the future, like the past, would be present to its eyes." Such a mind would possess a complete knowledge of the universe.[18]

On the contrary, however, far from revealing the whole history of the world, Laplace's theory would not let us know that there was a world at all. As Polanyi says, Laplace assumes that "we should explain all kinds of experience *in terms of atomic data*." Once you refuse to make this fallacious assumption, however, "you immediately see that Laplacean mind understands precisely nothing and that whatever it knows means precisely nothing."[19]

Yet it is this type of thinking that makes the community a collection of individuals, the living body a collection of cells, and the cell a collection of atoms. It is capable of regarding a human being as nothing more than a highly complicated chemical compound and the human mind as a mere sum total of its contents. Nominalism does not stop with the individual substance but goes on to dissolve it, too. Its urge to analyze and to synthesize mechanically reduces a substance to its elementary components, which it never succeeds in putting together again in their original form because it sees the whole only as an assembly of parts.

The nominalist mind therefore cannot understand a natural whole or appreciate a natural good. To illustrate what is meant by this, let us make an assertion: the life of the mosquito is a good to the mosquito. But of course; the mosquito has a subjective urge that makes it fly away when it sees a hand raised to swat it. Very well, let us substitute another proposition: the life of a tree is a good to the tree.

The tree has no subjective urges, so far as we can tell. It feels neither pleasure nor pain and makes no resistance to the woodsman when he cuts it down. But it is a single, unified organism, all of whose functions serve its life as this unfolds itself in a process of growth, development, and eventual reproduction. Although the tree knows nothing of good or evil, its life is its good because its being and its intelligibility consist in its life. The tree cannot be understood, simply as a fact, unless it is understood as an organic whole, organized for life and growth, not for disease and death.

That all trees eventually die is irrelevant, since a tree cannot be said for that reason to be intrinsically indifferent to life and death. Like all material and composite things, it will finally decompose. But what makes it a tree, so long as it remains one, is its unifying inner thrust toward living, not the fact that it will someday die. Nor does one dispose of the organic unity of a tree by asserting that trees are the products of a blind, mechanical evolution. What evolves is more significant than how it evolves, and the "how" does not explain away the "what."[20] No matter how they came to be here, while there are trees on earth, they are living organisms whose lives are the ends which their intrinsic functions serve.

That is why it is possible to speak of a particular tree as deformed, diseased, or dying. The being of a tree is a standard by which its good or ill can be judged. The good spoken of here is not a moral but an ontological one. But it is a true, objective, and intellectually knowable good, founded in the recognition of a tree as a natural whole. When we turn our attention to those natural wholes called human beings, we may recognize that they, too, have an ontological good proper to their nature. It is this good that makes moral judgments by and about human beings possible.

All of this is difficult for the nominalist mind to grasp because it seeks to understand and explain everything in terms of its parts and therefore overlooks the priority of the whole of which they are parts. Because it is antipathetic to the idea of natural wholes, such a mind also finds it hard to entertain the notion of relations as natural. For it, relations are external, accidental, and adventitious, not consequences of the natures of things. Reality is made up of individual things that collide with one another to form more or less lasting patterns. These patterns are the only order of nature that there is.

This conception of reality has led to the understanding of relations among human beings as external and voluntary. The individual human being is an atom, motivated by self-interest, to whom violence is done if he is subjected to a relationship with other humans which he has not chosen. It is no accident that this mentality thinks of civil society as essentially contractual, that its corrosive view of community is now affecting marriage and the family (to the point of contractualizing the relations among parents and children), and that it seeks to reduce the two sexes so far as possible into one, relations among whose members will be a matter of freely chosen lifestyles.

It is understandable, therefore, that thinkers infected or affected by nominalism should regard all goods as subjective, that is, as objects of desires or as what positivism calls "values." One may not know whether the cause of pleasure or pain is objectively good or evil. One may doubt whether objective good and evil are meaningful terms at all. But one can be certain of pleasure and pain precisely because they are so totally subjective; one feels them or one does not.

A politics based upon the pleasure-pain principle must be one that seeks to satisfy the most basic human drives. (Whether they will be the desires of the ruling few or of the democratic many then becomes the primary issue of politics.) The early modern period took greed and the desire for power as the strongest of these drives. "Men pursue their ends, which are wealth and power," as Machiavelli almost casually remarked.[21] Hobbes for his part took as "a general inclination of all mankind, a perpetual and restless desire of power after power, that ceaseth only in death."[22] But these writers did not see what was lacking in their view of the moving forces of human nature.

One of our own contemporaries has pointed it out. "If a leading insight of modernity was that men do badly so long as they try to stifle rather than to compound with the passions," says Joseph Cropsey, "then surely the modern project must be said to have lain in a state of incipience until the sexual appetite, as well as those more visibly political ones disencumbered by Machiavelli and Hobbes, was itself at last reported on the surface."[23]

Now that it has been reported on the surface, our nominalism forbids us to think of it in terms of natural purpose and function, and our individualistic hedonism compels us to leave the judgment on satisfying it to each man's taste, "so long as he doesn't hurt anyone else." Hence follow a number of contemporary trends, one of which is public tolerance of pornography as the sign by which one may know that he is in a liberal democracy. The reader may decide for himself whether this situation represents liberalism's finest hour or its most fetid flower.

Even if it is the flower, however, it is only the flower and not the root. It is worth calling attention to merely because its odor may cause people to wonder about its root. Then they may address themselves to the more serious matter of how long a society and a culture can maintain themselves on the basis of the subjectivity of values.

Notes

1. University of California Publications in Political Science (1943, reprinted New York: Howard Fertig, 1971).

2. Ibid., 5, 35–36, 9.

3. Ibid., 10, 50.

4. For an exposition of this view see Frank M. Coleman, "The Hobbesian Basis of American Constitutionalism," *Polity* 7 (1974): 67–74, with further references in n. 27.

5. *Politics and Vision* (Boston: Little, Brown and Company, 1969), 293.

6. *Leviathan*, ed. with intro. by Michael Oakeshott (Oxford: Blackwell, n.d.), chap. 15, p. 104.

7. *Essay concerning Human Understanding*, bk. 2, chap. 20, sect. 2, in *The Works of John Locke*, 10 vols. (London: Thomas Tegg et al., 1823, reprinted by Scientia Verlag Aalen, Germany, 1963) 1: 231.

8. *An Introduction to the Principles of Morals and Legislation in The Works of Jeremy Bentham*, 11 vols., reproduced from the Bowring Edition of 1838–43 (New York: Russell & Russell, 1962) 1: 1.

9. Ed. Oskar Piest (Indianapolis: The Library of Liberal Arts, Bobbs-Merrill Co., 1957), 45, 48, 49.

10. *Leviathan*, chap. 15, p. 104.

11. See John Dunn, *The Political Thought of John Locke* (Cambridge: Cambridge University Press, 1969), 187.

12. *Anarchical Fallacies*, in *Works* 2: 501.

13. Hobbes, *Leviathan*, intro., lv. The second of the nominalist doctrines, that will is precedent to reason in both God and man, is a consequence of the first doctrine, that the reality of a thing is its individuality.

14. Locke says all of this so often that it is almost otiose to give references, but see bk. 4, chap. 3, sect. 23 in Works 2: 374; 2, 1, 2, in 1: 83; 4, 6, 11, in 3: 7: 2, 23, 32, in 2: 30; 2, 31, 6–13, in 2: 129–35; 3, 3, 20, in 2: 185; 3, 3, 11, in 2: 72.

15. *English Political Thought in the 19th Century* (New York: Harper & Bros., 1962), 16.

16. *The Philosophy of J. S. Mill* (Oxford: Clarendon Press, 1953), 119–21, 181–82, 173.

17. *Preliminary Discourse to the Encyclopedia of Diderot*, trans. and ed. Richard N. Schwab (Indianapolis: The Library of Liberal Arts, Bobbs-Merrill Co., 1963), 22.

18. *Personal Knowledge* (New York and Evanston: Harper & Row, 1964), 139–40.

19. Ibid., 141.

20. It is of course questionable whether we can explain living organic matter by a blind, mechanical development of its chemical composition. Be that as it may, all we need insist on here is that an organism cannot be understood as a mere sum of its parts. It is intelligible only as a composite but single, living whole.

21. *The Ruler: A Modern Translation of Il Principe* (Chicago: Henry Regnery Co., 1955), chap. 25, p. 123.

22. *Leviathan*, chap. 11, p. 64.

23. *Political Philosophy and the Issues of Politics* (Chicago: University of Chicago Press, 1977), 316.

12

Brief Essays on Liberalism and Liberty

Dissolving the Norms

Any society with clear and strong moral standards breeds hypocrites. Unwilling or unable to live up to the socially approved norms, they pretend to do so for fear of public opprobrium. Hypocrisy is the tribute vice pays to virtue, but the hypocrites understandably resent having to pay it.

They have two avenues of escape from their uncomfortable situation. One is to change their lives and begin to practice what society preaches. The other and easier course is to undermine society's standards. In a society such as ours, which is losing confidence in its right to make moral judgments, the easy way out has become a broad highway crowded with people seeking relief from all moral rules that are not of their own choosing.

The attack on social moral standards is most obvious at the present time in the demand for "gay rights" laws. The demand succeeds as often as it does because in this country's current egalitarian mood it is hard to mobilize public sentiment against laws that only seem to forbid discrimination. But the thrust of these antidiscrimination laws is toward a deep change in social morality.

A columnist in New York's *Village Voice* has explained that the seemingly moderate campaign for an end to discrimination against homosexuals "has radical potential, because civil rights legislation opens the way to acceptance, and acceptance opens the way to dissolution of the norm." Dissolving the norm in regard to sexual conduct is the real object of the "gay rights" movement. Its purpose is to get society to

Pins in the Liberal Balloon (1990)

125

agree that, in the words of another columnist, homosexuality is just another way of living and AIDS is just another way of dying.

Once society accepts this claim, further questions arise. Why, for instance, are homosexuals not allowed to marry one another? Syndicated columnist Beverly Stephen has raised this question in what may be the opening salvo of a barrage on the civil rights front.

The present structure of American marriage law, weakened though it has been in recent decades, is still heavily biased in favor of lifelong union between one man and one woman. The law thus expresses a social judgment in favor of one way of life as against other ways, establishes a legally privileged position for heterosexual monogamy, and discriminates against people who engage in other forms of sexual union. This bias in the law deprives homosexuals of legal rights which they could enjoy if only they could get married.

Ms. Stephen explains: "By law, married heterosexuals have inheritance rights, tax benefits, Social Security benefits, access to a spouse's insurance coverage, and rights to make medical decisions or funeral arrangements." Unmarried couples who live together have none of these rights, but if they are heterosexuals they at least can get married. A homosexual couple cannot, and that's not fair. Ergo, we must dissolve the heterosexual norm of marriage so that everyone may enjoy equal rights.

Now, Beverly Stephen is no more an Important Thinker than you or I, and there is no need to panic merely because she has floated an idea. Still, she has allies in the upper echelons of serious thought. Bruce A. Ackerman, who is a professor of law and philosophy at Columbia University, presumably is an important thinker. At least *The Chronicle of Higher Education* takes him as one in a recent article on the revival of political philosophy. What Professor Ackerman thinks is that "our fundamental right is the right to go to hell in our own way."

Society, for Ackerman and other highly regarded academics, exists in order to protect that right; society therefore may not impose norms that impair it. Here we see the real issue that faces American society. Beneath the surface phenomena of struggles over civil rights laws, affirmative action programs, and equal protection litigation, beneath the shouting about discrimination, censorship, and "imposing values" is the question whether society can and should maintain any moral norms at all.

There are those who want to dissolve the norms in the name of liberty and equality in a pluralistic society. It becomes steadily more clear, however, that the basic premise of their argument is what George Will has aptly called the moral equality of appetites. The original American proposition was that all men are created equal and are endowed by their Creator with certain unalienable rights. Now the proposition is that all persons are equally entitled to the satisfaction of their several preferences, urges, and drives. Because the persons are equal, their appetites are equally worthy of society's moral respect and the law's protection.

Some like chocolate, some like vanilla. Some like Mozart, other prefer heavy metal. Some like girls, some like boys. Some love God, others hate Him. It is all the same because man is a bundle of desires and each man strives to satisfy the desires that he has. Society's only task is to preside over the striving with impartial neutrality so that we can all live together in peace.

I am reminded of a billboard that I often saw during World War II. It bore the picture of a particularly stupid-looking G.I., with his fatigue cap on backward, who proclaimed, "I'm fighting for my right to boo the Dodgers." But no one fights for his right to boo the Dodgers. If you fight, you might get hurt or even killed, and in your right mind you will not risk life and limb for the sake of booing a baseball team. Nor, we may suspect, will many fight to defend an idea of liberty that dissolves every social norm worth living by or dying for.

Liberty, Equality, and Order

Liberty, equality, fraternity was the slogan of the French Revolution. Liberty and equality were the Revolution's operative goals, and fraternity was brought in as a cement to hold them together. For liberty and equality are not necessarily in harmony and, in fact, are often at war with each other. Keeping the peace between them therefore became the role of fraternity. Alas, fraternity has not been terribly successful at it, as the history of class struggle since the French Revolution has shown.

In the evolution of democratic theory in the past two centuries, two main currents have emerged from the same wellspring of radical individualism: the liberal stream, emphasizing liberty while acknowledging equality of civil rights, and the egalitarian stream, emphasizing equality while preaching the liberty guaranteed by civil rights.

Liberal democracy understands rights as immunities from governmental interference. Their function is to prevent government from unduly restraining any individual's liberty. The egalitarian conception of rights is much broader than the classical liberal one and includes a wide range of positive benefits to be conferred by government. It tends toward an equality of results rather than merely of opportunities. To put it crudely, it means not only that you are free to apply for the job, but that you get it and you keep it.

Liberal democratic thought has as its economic counterpart the ideology of capitalism and a free-market economic system. The egalitarian stream ushers in the ideology of socialism and a government dedicated to bringing about substantial economic equality among all citizens.

Liberalism as it exists in the United States today is an effort to have the best of both ideological worlds. It assigns to government the duty of fostering, not complete economic equality, but general prosperity and a more equal share in it for all citizens. At the same time, through an ever-expanding array of civil rights, it seeks to emancipate the individual from religious, moral, and social restraints that are not of his own choosing. The contemporary liberal ideal would be a country in which everyone was employed at high wages in work which he/she found fulfilling, without distinction of race, color, creed, gender, ethnic origin, educational background, or sexual preference, and could live by any "lifestyle" that he/she chose.

Contemporary American conservatism is largely a reaction to this brand of liberalism, and therefore is a mixed bag of views. Among its adherents we find "conservatives" who are really nineteenth-century liberals eager to get government off the back of business. We also find "social-issue" conservatives angered by the liberal dissolution of our public morality. Still others are "libertarians" who want no public morality at all but oppose liberalism because of the large role it gives government. Another group of conservatives are regionalists or "states-righters" who are against not government as such, but the federal government.

The ideological conflict between and among liberals and conservatives is carried on in terms of liberty and equality. We all agree that all men are created equal and are endowed by their Creator with certain inalienable rights, among which are life, liberty, and the pursuit of happiness. Even if we leave the Creator out of the discussion—because He is "divisive" and so best not talked about in a pluralistic society—we still agree that we are equal and somehow endowed with inalienable rights.

Our political disputes consequently have a way of becoming arguments about rights. We operate in this country on what the late Alexander Bickel called a "liberal contractarian model" of society, which "rests on a vision of individual rights that have a clearly defined, independent existence predating society and are derived from nature and from a natural, if imagined, contract. Society must bend to these rights.''[1] All that is left to argue about is what the rights are, in the possession of which we are all equal. Clearly defined though the rights are assumed to be, we in fact do not agree on what is included in them.

To that question there is no answer in terms of liberty and equality alone. Without some ordering principle that specifies the content of liberty and equality, we cannot harmonize the two goals. The ordering principle, to work effectively, must be outside of and above liberty and equality. It cannot be a vague ''fraternity'' but must be some commonly held judgment on what human beings are and what is truly good for them.

The mere thought of such a common moral principle superior to liberty and equality makes the contemporary liberal mind—and some conservative minds—shudder. We lack such an ordering principle because we are so devoted to liberty and equality as the supreme norms of a democratic society that we will not admit their subordination to any higher norms.

Yet liberty and equality cannot be the highest values of a political system because they relativize and ultimately destroy all other values. When we make them our supreme norms, we have no set of objectively valid human ends that can provide answers to the questions, Liberty for what? and Equality in what? We therefore cannot have the communal beliefs without which in the long run there is no community.

We have no firm basis on which such societal values as we happen to hold at a particular time can be transmitted from generation to generation. Even the most devout among us are prone to consider their moral convictions as merely private beliefs. Their children become unthinking moral relativists, as many a teacher today can testify.

In short, American society now lacks what Walter Lippmann called the public philosophy. We shall lack it increasingly as the moral and religious capital of our culture, on which liberalism has always traded even as it eroded it, is drained away. We are left with an unending battle between conflicting claims to liberty and equality, and no publicly acknowledged principle with which to resolve the conflict.

Rights as the Beginning and End

I was paging through the *New York Times Book Review*, as is my wont of a Sunday afternoon, when my eye was caught by a brief, unsigned review of yet another book on abortion. According to the review, the author of the book concludes that, while the fetus has a right to life from the moment of conception, "this right to live does not entitle the fetus to use a woman's body against her will."

The issue, one notices, is posed in terms of rights and entitlements. "May I use your body, madam?" "Yes, dear, of course you may" or "No, you are not entitled to it and anyhow, I don't want you." Such language does not surprise us in a liberal society that thinks habitually in terms of rights. Yet even in a liberal society one must wonder by what tortuous mental process a man comes to discuss the morality of destroying human life as though he were a lawyer arguing a case of trespass on private property.

The fetus is cast as the party of the first part who pleads his right to live, which he cannot sustain without a temporary lease of the woman's body. She is the party of the second part who asserts an absolute property right to her own body. The court must decide which of these rights should prevail. Since the fetus, when all is said and done, is an intruder on someone else's property, he loses. That what he loses is his life may be regrettable, but the superior right has prevailed and so justice has been done.

But how does one come to think of the beginning of human life and the morality of ending it in these terms? The answer, I believe, is that one is an intellectual heir of John Locke and therefore thinks of a human being as essentially an individual proprietor.

In this view, each man is an island, of which he is the sole owner. He owns his body, the actions he performs with it, and the goods he acquires by those actions. In Locke's terminology, he is endowed by nature with original rights to life, liberty, and estate, which collectively form his "property." His only obligation is to respect the equal rights of other persons, all of whom are individual proprietors like himself.

Since disputes over rights inevitably arise, these proprietors enter into a social contract with each other, by which they form a civil society and set up a government with authority to resolve conflicts of rights. The contract into which individuals have freely entered obliges them to accept the government's decision in such cases.

But they remain what they were by nature: individuals distinct and separate from one another, each the owner of his own life, liberty, and estate. The relationship they have formed with one another by joining together in society is artificial, external, and contractual; it is not rooted in their nature as social beings. They formed the relationship so that each one could better protect his individual proprietary rights, and society's government has no function other than to protect those rights.

In the same spirit, the leaders of the French Revolution proclaimed in their Declaration of the Rights of Man and the Citizen that "ignorance, neglect, or contempt of the rights of men are the sole causes of public misfortunes and corruptions of Government." Implicit in this remarkable assertion is the proposition that if we only get our conception of rights straight and implement it in practice, we shall have solved all the problems of society and accomplished all the legitimate purposes of government.

This attitude prevails in influential circles in America today. Philosophers begin their political theories with the individual self and then seek to show how it can be incorporated into society without compromising its selfhood. Novelists depict and sometimes celebrate the war of the self against the restraints of society's culture. Newspapers and magazines, as the discerning reader will notice, often translate issues that affect all of society into struggles between conflicting rights.

Thus, for example, school busing becomes a conflict between the right of black parents to send their children to an integrated school and the right of white parents to send their children to a neighborhood school. Pornography is regarded not as a social problem, but as a conflict between the right of some people to have access to "adult" material and the right of others not to have the same material thrown in their faces. Even what to do about AIDS turns into a debate about rights.

The question, however, is not whether human beings have rights; they do, and few today will question that. Rather it is what model or picture of society should guide our thinking. In one model, which comes down to us from Aristotle and Aquinas, we think of man as a social being from whose nature flow relations to his family, neighbors, fellow workers, the community, and the political order. These relations are the foundation of both rights and obligations that are prior to and independent of consent. In the Lockean model we conceive of man as an independent proprietor whose social relations are only those to which he has freely consented.

Individualists understandably prefer the second model, and the American Civil Liberties Union is hopelessly in love with it, but it leads to strange and distorted conclusions about social reality. If we take the principles of liberal individualism as axiomatic, we find it possible to think of the fetus and the woman as the parties of the first and second part arguing over their respective rights. We are then able to blind ourselves to the natural fact that they are related as mother and child and that the child is in the only natural place for him to be, his mother's womb.

The Rot in Liberal Politics

Even liberals are beginning to notice what is wrong with liberalism. In a perceptive article which appeared in the liberal Catholic journal *Commonweal* (January 13, 1989), Fred Siegel put his finger on contemporary liberalism's Achilles' heel. "Liberalism," he says, "has a proud history of defending individual rights. . . . But liberalism, wrapped as it is in the defense of personal autonomy, is unable to speak to the social breakdown which increasingly plagues us. It is mute before abuses of liberty."

"The law," he explains, "once the cornerstone of ordered liberty, has been trivialized, turned into a game for lawyers." There has been "a decisive break between New Deal liberalism, whose mild economic egalitarianism was based on a sense of shared values, and the moral relativism of post–New Deal liberalism which is grounded in individually held rights. Those assertions of rights which serve to trump the claims of a common morality make it difficult and often impossible for cultural liberals to pass judgment on even the most obviously destructive behavior."

There, he says, we may find a major reason for the Democratic Party's defeat in the last presidential election. Since 1968 the party has been preoccupied with procedural rules designed to guarantee proportional representation to all of its constituent groups, however out of harmony with the general electorate they may be. But this preoccupation with procedures is "a means of avoiding a consensus on at least a core of substantive issues. In that sense the Democratic Party's proceduralism is a faithful reflection of contemporary liberalism's unwillingness to pass judgment on what is or isn't good."

Mr. Siegel's purpose in that article was to warn liberals that they are killing the Democratic Party's chances in national elections. But the rot now so apparent in liberal politics was planted in liberal social and political theory at its beginning, more than three centuries ago. Liberalism in its classical form was, and remains today, a radically individualistic philosophy. Even when it veers toward the welfare state or democratic socialism, it does so in order to equalize everyone's chance to live the lifestyle of his choice. It has no theory of what is a good life for human beings as such.

I read somewhere, not long ago, that liberalism's great accomplishments were to break the power of absolute monarchs, thus bringing governments under law, and to establish religious freedom. One could point out that constitutionalism, the doctrine that government is limited by law, is far older than the rise of liberalism in the seventeenth century. It was in the thirteenth century that Bracton wrote, "The king is under no man, but under God and the law," and that idea was already old when he wrote. But it is true historically that modern conceptions of limited, constitutional government and of religious liberty triumphed in the modern world under the aegis of liberalism.

But much as we may applaud the historical achievements of liberalism, we must also recognize that one of its consequences has been the steady relativization of the ideas of truth and moral good, and that this was a consequence implicit in liberal individualism from the beginning. For multitudes today, truth is only what the individual thinks is true, good is only what the individual personally prefers, and justice is his right to act on his preferences, so long as they are compatible with the equal right of others to do the same.

That is currently the liberal model of society, and it is falling apart. Constitutional democracy clearly needs a better theoretical foundation than liberal individualism.

It is not that a sounder theory of democracy has yet to be written. We may find powerful essays toward it in John Hallowell's *Moral Foundation of Democracy*, Yves Simon's *Philosophy of Democratic Government*, Jacques Maritain's *Man and the State*, and a host of other books. The major task remaining to us is to persuade the rest of the population—particularly academics, journalists, and lawyers—to stop taking liberalism with its individualism, its relativism, and its assertion of rights that trump the claims of a common morality, as the necessary foundation of democracy. Liberalism, which we may credit with beginning its career as the political philosophy of freedom, has blossomed into mere permissiveness, and is now a menace rather than a support of constitutional democracy.

Ordered Liberty

I once read somewhere that the trouble with liberals is that they have not yet noticed the twentieth century. That is still true of by far the greater number of them. But as our century staggers to its close, some of them are beginning to take note of it.

The New Republic, for instance, which is certifiably liberal, remarked in an editorial on February 8, 1988, on liberal blindness to "cultural decline." Liberals, it said, do not want to see this unpleasant reality because it "challenges their own attachment to the endlessness of personal freedoms. . . . Contemporary liberalism is so intellectually and psychologically invested in the doctrine of ever-expanding rights—the rights of privacy, the rights of children, the rights of criminals, the rights of pornographers, the rights of everyone to everything—that any suggestions of the baleful consequences of that doctrine appears to them as a threat to the liberal idea itself.''

Whether it is a threat depends on what one thinks is ''the liberal idea itself.'' Liberalism as a theory of ethics and politics lasted as long as it did and worked as well as it did because it assumed that rational and decent people would see the difference between moral right and wrong and would for the most part respect it. Liberalism, however, was able to do this because it incorporated into its idea of personal freedom moral norms that it did not create but inherited from the classical and Christian past.

As liberals have used up this moral capital, they have come to regard these or any other transcendent moral norms as threats to the liberal idea itself. They may well be right, too, because the core of liberalism has always been the autonomy of the individual and his right to decide for himself which norms he will obey.

Those who think that today's liberals are wrong—as *The New Republic* does when it proposes ''the subtle truth that it really is wise restraints that make us genuinely free''—will have to revise the liberal idea of freedom. Above all, they will have to remove from the core of liberalism the belief that liberty consists in the sovereignty of the individual and his indefeasible right to decide for himself. More than two hundred years ago Edmund Burke put the key question: ''Even in matters which are, as it were, just within our reach, what would become of the world, if the practice of all moral duties, and the foundations of society, rested upon having their reasons made clear and demonstrative to every individual?''[2]

A sounder idea of freedom is contained in the phrase ordered liberty, of which the U.S. Supreme Court has become fond. Despite the bizarre implications the Court has found in it (abortion on demand, for example), the phrase in itself is a good one and, properly used, could provide an antidote to the corrosive acid of individualism.

To quote Burke once again (he was speaking of the British constitution, but his words will apply to our own as well), ''The distinguishing part of our constitution is its liberty. . . . But the liberty, the only liberty I mean, is a liberty connected with order; that not only exists along with order and virtue, but which cannot exist at all without them.''[3]

The order without which liberty cannot exist has several levels. It is a legal and political order, a social order, and a cultural order constituted by commonly held conventions, codes of manners, moral principles, and beliefs about the nature of man and his place in the world. At its deepest level, it rests on belief in divine revelation, or on the conviction that the order of creation is open and accessible to human reason, or on both together. Ordered liberty depends upon an ordered universe.

It cannot be produced by a merely fabricating reason that tries to construct its own order out of its desires. Ordered liberty must be based on principles outside of and higher than our passions, as Burke explained: "Men are qualified for civil liberty in exact proportion to their disposition to put moral chains upon their own appetites. . . . Society cannot exist unless a controlling power upon will and appetite be placed somewhere, and the less of it there is within, the more there must be without. It is ordained in the eternal constitution of things that men of intemperate mind cannot be free. Their passions forge their fetters."[4]

It is the nature of our freedom that, if we abuse it, we lose it. This result is obvious in the case of persons who become enslaved to alcohol, drugs, gambling, or other addictions. But the pride, greed, lust, anger, envy, gluttony, and sloth with which we are all infected also forge fetters that are no less fetters for being called rights. Hence our need for "wise restraints that genuinely make us free," and the further need to recognize an overarching moral order from which we may learn what restraints are truly wise.

This idea will not sit well with liberals who believe in "the rights of everyone to everything." As Burke said of their French revolutionary forebears, "The little catechism of the rights of men is soon learned, and the inferences are in the passions."[5] But if neither reason nor revelation is permitted to furnish us with standards by which to distinguish spurious from valid claims to rights, all such claims must be mere assertions of the individual's passionate desires.

This conclusion, however, leads to the attempt, characteristic of contemporary liberalism, to found the order of law and politics on equal respect for the passions of all individuals. Gorge Sabine, somewhere in his *History of Political Theory*, described what lies at the end of that road: "The absolutely sovereign and omnicompetent state is the logical correlate of a society which consists of atomic individuals." Such a state need not be a brutal dictatorship. It could be a bureaucratic despotism operating on the principles of the American Civil Liberties Union.

Notes

1. *The Morality of Consent* (New Haven: Yale University Press, 1975), 4.
2. *A Vindication of Natural Society in The Works of the Right Honourable Edmund Burke*, 16 vols. (London: Rivington, 1803–27) 1: 7.
3. *Speech at His Arrival at Bristol*, 1774, in *Works* 3: 8.
4. *Letter to a Member of the National Assembly* in *Works*, 6: 64.
5. *Thoughts on French Affairs*, in *Works* 7: 42.

13

Government, Individualism, and Mediating Communities

We have in this country a pluralistic society, and one that is becoming more pluralistic all the time. This pluralistic society is organized and governed under a constitutional liberal democracy. There are three terms in that phrase: democratic, liberal, and constitutional. Of these three terms, the most important is constitutional.

What is constitutionalism? It is not by definition liberalism or democracy. There could be, and historically there have been, constitutional governments that were not democratic and not necessarily liberal. What constitutionalism means is simply limited government. If government is limited in its power and in its functions, it is a constitutional government. That does not necessarily imply a written constitution. As Americans, we think it does. But Great Britain has not had a single document that one can point to and say, that is the British constitution. Constitutionalism simply means the idea of limited government and, therefore, a society that is free precisely because the powers of government are limited.

The limits on government are three: legal, political, and social. First, the legal limits on government. Forty years ago Professor Charles McIlwain of Harvard, who was the leading authority on the history of political thought in his day, explained, ''In all its successive phases, constitutionalism has had one essential quality: it is a legal limitation on government; it is the antithesis of arbitrary rule; its opposite is despotic government, the government of will instead of law. . . . but the most ancient, the most persistent, and the most lasting of the essentials of

Delivered at Allies for Faith and Renewal conference (1988)

true constitutionalism still remains what it has been almost from the beginning: the limitation of government by law.''[1] But that is not the only limitation on government.

There is the political limitation. Government is limited when it needs to get the consent of the people to what it does. The people need not be the entire population. Certainly in eighteenth-century Britain the politically effective people were not the entire population or even a very large part of it. But there was an elected House of Commons. This connoted the ability of the people legally and peacefully to change the personnel of government. As McIlwain pointed out, government, earlier in the Middle Ages, was considered to be limited government, but unfortunately, there was no legal way to enforce the limits on it. The barons had to get together at Runnymede, put their lances on King John's chest, and say, "Sign here." And then, under compulsion, he signed Magna Carta.

The political limitation on government means that the people through the process of election can change the personnel of government. When we extend the notion of the people to include the entire adult population, then we have democracy and, combined with legal limits on the powers of government, it is a constitutional democracy.

The third limit on the power of government is a social one. It resides in the existence of institutions that government did not create, but whose rights and influence it must respect. There are many things that a government in Washington will not try to do if big business, big agriculture, and big labor, or any two of them, seriously object to them. These are among the so-called mediating or intermediary institutions that stand as a check upon the power of government and, therefore, as a guarantee of the freedom of the people. The most important mediating institution is the family. Among the others are churches, professional associations, labor unions, businesses, service organizations, and a free press.

Modern liberal constitutional thought, which had its origins in the seventeenth century, has tended from its beginning to limit the powers of government by guaranteeing the rights of individuals. But what people do and the theory by which they explain it to themselves and others are not one and the same thing. Liberalism developed as an ideology to justify and explain what liberal constitutionalists were trying to do, namely, to limit and control the power of the Crown. Since the ideology they framed to achieve this, however, was flawed and defective, certain ill consequences have followed from it.

In fashioning it, liberal theorists hypothesized a state of nature populated by independent individuals, in which there was no civil society under government and law. But this "state of nature" inevitably degenerated into a state of anarchy because everyone was a judge in his own cause whenever there was a dispute over conflicting interpretations of rights. Men then formed a social contract to set up a government that would settle disputes and protect rights. Its only purpose was to protect the rights of individuals. For the rest, they were free to pursue their own goals.

That view was a break with the medieval conception of constitutionalism, which limited the power of the king by his subjection to age-old law. In the Middle Ages, the law was customary law. No one made it. It had always been there "since the mind of man runneth not to the contrary," and it was superior to king and people alike. The other check on the power of kings in the Middle Ages was the rights and powers of the Church, the nobility, the universities, the chartered towns, and the holders of property. These were the intermediary institutions whose rights the king had to respect.

But from the late Middle Ages on, as we have seen, political theory focused increasingly on drawing the line between the state and the individual. Recent constitutional law in the United States has limited government by insisting more and more upon individual rights. Still more recently, so has civil rights legislation enacted by Congress or by the several state legislatures. This undoubtedly limits what government may do to individuals, but by the same token, and necessarily, it increases what government may do for individuals and to institutions.

Consequently, government today is obligated to be, at one and the same time, individualistic and statist. It is individualistic when it serves an expanding array of individual rights. But insofar as it uses the power of the state to impose these rights upon institutions, government is statist, and the fingers of the bureaucracy reach more and more into all of the institutions of society.

Stanley Hauerwas already has been quoted as saying, "It is the strategy of liberalism to ensure the existence of the autonomy of cultural and economic life by ensuring the freedom of the individual. Ironically, that strategy results in the undermining of intermediate institutions, because they are now understood only as those arbitrary institutions sustained by the private desires of individuals." But, as he also said, whatever else the family is, it is not simply a voluntary institution.[2]

In one sense marriage obviously is voluntary. No one has to get married. If one does marry, he is not obliged to marry this one rather than that one. John marries Mary because John and Mary consent to marry each other. Their consent constitutes the marriage. But what they consent to is marrying one another; they do not determine what marriage is.

They cannot marry for a year and a day, or establish a married ménage à trois, or marry persons of the same sex as themselves. It is true that the state could legalize any of these arrangements and give it the same status as marriage. But by so doing the state would undermine and ultimately destroy a relationship founded on the nature of man, woman, and the family which, whether we care to admit it or not, is a given natural reality and not merely the object of private desires. As Hauerwas said, by our insistence on seeing the private rights of individuals as the only check on the power of the state, we are seriously weakening marriage and the other basic institutions of society as well.

Let me offer a few instances of this out of many that one could recite. One is the Grove City case. Grove City College is a small, private, liberal arts college in Pennsylvania. It had steadfastly refused to accept any federal funds, one reason being that Title IX of the Education Act of 1972 requires a school, if it receives federal funds, to comply with federal regulations issued under the Education Act that ban various forms of discrimination.

The bureaucratic agency of the government that was concerned with administering these regulations wrote to Grove City College and told its administrators that they were obliged to fill out forms saying that they had complied with the requirements of this act. One of the complaints against them was that they had practiced sex discrimination by insisting that young men and young women play on separate teams in athletic sports. Grove City replied that it did not have to comply, because it had not received federal money. The bureaucrats said that it had received federal funds because it had students who had student loans and grants. This put federal money into the college, and therefore it was obliged by the act.

The case went to court, and the Supreme Court decided, in Solomonic fashion, to split the baby in two. That is to say, the Court decided that Grove City College was indeed obliged by the act to the extent that the federal funds coming into the school affected its programs. But since the funds were in the form of student aid, they would affect only the admissions office and the financial aid office, and nothing else in the school.

For four years after that decision various civil rights groups labored to get Congress to pass a law clarifying the meaning of the 1972 act. Congress obliged by passing the Civil Rights Restoration Act of 1988.

This act says that if a private institution (it need not be a school; it could be a hospital or an orphanage) receives federal money in any way, it is obliged to comply with all the regulations issued under the various civil rights laws passed by Congress.

Once a law is passed, it gets out of the hands of Congress and is turned over to the administrative agencies, the bureaucracy, which then spell out its meaning by issuing guidelines or regulations. If an institution wants to contest them, it has to go to court and persuade the court that the federal regulations are not what Congress intended. There thus is a transfer of power from the legislative branch of the government, i.e., the Congress, to the executive, or administrative branch, and ultimately, to the judicial branch.

There was no great public reaction against the Civil Rights Restoration Act. President Ronald Reagan vetoed it and it went back to Congress. At this point evangelical groups woke up and began to deluge Congress with protests urging Congress not to override the president's veto. But as *Time* magazine remarked, even Republicans did not dare to vote against anything called a civil rights act in an election year and, of course, the Democrats voted for it because among their important constituent groups are precisely the people who wanted this kind of law. Congress passed the act over the president's veto, and the result is a further extension of federal power into private institutions in this country.

An even more extreme example is the Georgetown University case, which involved one of the many of the gay rights laws that have been passed in cities in this country. For instance, a year or two ago the mayor of New York, by executive order, told all church-related agencies performing services for the city under contract—such as running orphanages and foster care—that they would have to agree to nondiscrimination in the employment of homosexuals. The Catholic Church in New York was in an interregnum in which the previous archbishop had died and the new one had not been appointed; so it did nothing. But the Salvation Army stood up and said no, and the Jewish organization Agudath Israel did likewise. Finally, when Cardinal John O'Connor came in as archbishop of the Catholic archdiocese, he also refused to accept the mayor's order. These institutions went to court and got a declaration from the court that the mayor had acted beyond his power in issuing his executive order. He then got it through as an ordinance of the city council, but with an exception for the religious groups.

To return to the Georgetown University case, the District of Columbia passed an ordinance making it unlawful for an educational institution to deny access to any of its facilities and services to persons otherwise qualified—namely, students—for reasons based upon the race, color, religion, national origin, sex, age, marital status, personal appearance, sexual orientation, family responsibilities, political affiliations, source of income, or physical handicap of any individual.

Georgetown already had a homosexual students organization on campus. It is hard to prevent that. Any group of students can get together, and meet and talk with one another, and call themselves by whatever name they want. I do not see any effective way of stopping them from doing that. What a school can do is deny them official recognition as a student organization entitled to receive funds from the student government. That is what Georgetown did. The homosexual students then went to court under the District of Columbia ordinance. The university won in the trial court. That decision, however, was appealed to the Court of Appeals of the District of Columbia, the highest municipal court in the District, and it decided against the university.

The Georgetown administration, on its part, decided not to appeal this decision to the U.S. Supreme Court. I had hoped that it would go to the Supreme Court, so that, even if it lost there, it could tell the world, and its own alumni in particular, that it had fought the fight to the end and had had an unfavorable decision imposed upon it. Georgetown, however, did not take that step.

The president of Georgetown sent out a letter explaining why the administration did not carry the case to the Supreme Court. One reason was that Justice Antonin Scalia is a graduate of Georgetown and would therefore feel obliged to withdraw from decision of the case. That left the university facing the very real possibility of a 4–4 decision, which would leave the decision of the District Court of Appeals standing, with the apparent (though weak) approval of the Supreme Court of the United States.

Be that as it may, there is one line in the president's letter that is highly significant: "Despite the scattering of opinions in the Court of Appeals of the District of Columbia, the holding of the court is clear. The District of Columbia has a compelling interest in eradicating discrimination against homosexuals that overrides the First Amendment protection of Georgetown's religious objections to subsidizing homosexual organizations." Such are the priorities of a liberal egalitarian society, at least in the District of Columbia.

Decisions of the U.S. Supreme Court have also moved in the direction of immunizing the sexual freedom of individuals against the claims of intermediary institutions and of society at large. As we have already seen, in *Griswold v. Connecticut*,[3] the Supreme Court found in the Constitution a "right of privacy" which that document nowhere mentions, but which protected the marital relation against a state law forbidding the use of contraceptives. A subsequent decision extended this right of privacy to bar state interference with the sale and dissemination of contraceptives to unmarried persons.[4] *Roe v. Wade*[5] went on to find abortion to be another fundamental private right.

The Court has also added marriage to the list of constitutional rights not specified in the Constitution. In 1967, the Court struck down laws of the state of Virginia forbidding miscegenation, i.e., marriage between whites and blacks, on the ground that they deprived the parties to such marriages of the equal protection of the laws. At the very end of its opinion, however, the Court added that "the freedom to marry has long been recognized as one of the vital personal rights essential to the orderly pursuit of happiness by free men. . . . To deny this fundamental freedom on so insupportable a basis as the racial classifications embodied in these statutes, . . . is surely to deprive all the State's citizens of liberty without due process of law."[6] This statement was not necessary to the Court's decision of the case, but it transferred to the Court the final decision on what marriage is and in what ways the states may regulate it.

Presumably most of us will readily agree that there is a natural right to marry. But before we stand up and cheer for this new *constitutional* right, let us note that the Court has gone beyond freeing the right to marry from racial classifications. To give but one example, let us take the case of *Zablocki v. Redhail*.[7] The state of Wisconsin had a law providing that if a resident of the state had a minor child or children not in his custody and was under a court order to support them, he could not get a license to marry without showing that he had met his child-support obligation and that the children covered by that obligation were not and were not likely to become public charges. Under that law young Redhail was denied a license to marry.

As a high school student he had fathered an illegitimate baby girl, a fact that he admitted in court. He was put under a court order to contribute to his daughter's support but, being unemployed and indigent, he never did so, and the child became a public charge under the Aid to Families with Dependent Children program. When he applied for permission to marry another woman who was pregnant with a child by him, it was stipulated that, even if he had contributed the amount specified in the child-support order, his daughter would nonetheless have been a public charge. He was therefore denied permission to marry.

The U.S. Supreme Court, on appeal, declared the Wisconsin statute unconstitutional, not only as denying the equal protection of the laws, but as arbitrarily depriving Redhail and his bride-to-be "of a fundamental liberty protected by the Due Process Clause, the freedom to marry."[8] The Court explained:

> It would make little sense to recognize a right of privacy with respect to other matters of family life and not with respect to the decision to enter the relationship that is the foundation of the family in our society. The woman whom appellee [Redhail] desired to marry had a fundamental right to seek an abortion of their expected child, see *Roe v. Wade*, . . . , or to bring the child into life to suffer the myriad social, if not economic, disabilities that the status of illegitimacy brings, ... Surely a decision to marry and raise the child in a traditional family setting must receive equivalent protection.[9]

Let us forgo comment on the wisdom of the Wisconsin law or the evidence for Mr. Redhail's qualifications for raising a child in a traditional family setting. Here it is enough to call attention to the thoroughgoing individualism of the Court's opinion. The Court-created rights of the individual outweigh a mother's obligation to protect the life of the child in her womb, a father's obligation to support his earlier child, and society's interest in enforcing the duties that flow from those relationships.

We are confronted with a dilemma in this country, the dilemma of pluralism. There is no denying that we are a pluralistic society. Whether it is good, bad, or indifferent, it is a massive social fact, and there is no changing it, and any suggestions for changing it into something else are simply unrealistic. Furthermore, we are a democratic society, operating on the principle of the political equality of all citizens. That means that government must treat all citizens as equals before the law. But this principle is now widely taken to mean that government must be neutral toward all beliefs and preferences. In the eyes of the law, all convictions, all moral beliefs, are mere preferences, toward which government must be neutral.

At this conference the question has been asked: "How can we have any public morality when, by the mere fact that some significant minority objects to it, it is no longer public and, therefore, government may not stand behind it?" That, I think, pinpoints the real problem posed by the drift of our constitutional law and civil rights legislation at the present time. It comes down to a systematic denial that it is possible for the United States or any state of the union to have or uphold a public morality, because that would mean that government is imposing the morality of some upon others. It is quietly assumed that it is possible for a government to be neutral on all moral questions. The result is a steady lowering of the moral sights, imposed through antidiscrimination statutes and court decisions. The government and, in particular, the courts are put under constant pressure to intervene actively in private institutions in order to make them neutral.

I teach in a university, and I do not think its experience is different from that of any other university. I know that we can hardly make a move in a personnel case without the threat of a lawsuit. This has a distinctively chilling effect on our decisions. Some of our decisions may indeed be bad ones that should be chilled. But if you look at the overall effect of this constant threat of lawsuits upon the institution, it means that it progressively loses its independence.

The result is a bureaucratic state governing a flattened-out society in which people live in what Alexis de Tocqueville a hundred and fifty years ago called a "soft despotism," where the passion for equality abolishes liberty and with it, in the long run, pluralism. We then get what someone else has called the universal, homogeneous administrative state.

To conclude, I will make one overall suggestion: let us start to change our thinking. I am certainly in favor of both faith and renewal, an alliance that this conference has been assembled to encourage; but I would suggest that in regard to the evolving civil order, we learn to believe less and doubt more. Become very skeptical of the conventional wisdom. Do not let yourself be buffaloed. Do not let yourself be talked down. Ask questions such as "Why should we believe what you tell us?"

For example, we could begin by rethinking the individual versus the state as the necessary starting point of political theory. Instead, we could think of the political order as sustaining a community of communities—a new and better conception of pluralism. We could reject the notion that there is an irresolvable conflict between individual rights and public morality. I am certainly not denying or questioning the proposition that individual human beings have basic human rights. But they are *human* rights, not everyone's right to frame his own individual conception of morality. They are rights that must fit within some overarching community order, based upon some conception of what human beings are and what is good for human beings. We could then go on to make the strengthening of private institutions, the family in particular, the focus of public policy.

Suppose we were to say, "Yes, government is concerned with the welfare of all its people," but insofar as possible, it is going to pursue that welfare through strengthening, harmonizing, and if need be subsidizing private institutions that perform services of welfare to the community. Government will try especially to shore up, bolster, and strengthen the institution of the family as being the most basic transmitter of culture, of religion, and of the foundations of society.

Next, we could seek a better understanding of the phrase in the First Amendment, an "establishment of religion." The First Amendment has been in the Constitution since 1791, but the Supreme Court's interpretation of that clause is really only forty years old. It dates from the case of *Everson v. Board of Education* in 1947.[10] Prior to that decision, there were only three, possibly four, decisions of the Court interpreting the meaning of an establishment of religion, because the question seldom arose at the federal level. In 1947, the Court said that nonestablishment of religion is implicit in the Fourteenth Amendment and applies on the state level. That is the level on which the cases arise, primarily concerned with schools, but with other institutions also.

Since 1947 we have a whole body of case law interpreting "an establishment of religion." As Richard John Neuhaus recently remarked, this is largely the handiwork of one man, Leo Pfeffer, the general counsel of the American Jewish Congress, who, somewhat to his surprise, won case after case after case before the Supreme Court. Neuhaus said it was rather astonishing that he met with so little opposition. But Neuhaus has also mentioned that evangelical groups are now going to court aggressively and bringing cases to resist that interpretation of establishment. If that is true, I commend them. There ought to be more of that. I find it highly unfortunate that church-state relations have had to be fought out in the courts as interpretations of the Constitution, but if that is how they must be determined, let's get into the action and fight the fight.

I will end by quoting something that I read every time I pass through Washington Square in New York. At the top of the massive Washington Arch there is carved a passage from Washington's final words to the Constitutional Convention of 1787. They end with these lines: "Let us erect a standard to which the wise and honest may repair. The rest is in the hands of God."

We may well take those lines for our own motto. By all means let us strive to erect a standard to which the wise and honest may repair. But let us remember that the event is in the hands of God. We are not divine providence. It is not for us to plan history and make it come true. It is not in our power to save the United States. All that we can do is to carry out the will of God as He gives us to see that will, and leave the outcome to Him. He asks for nothing more.

Notes

1. *Constitutionalism, Ancient and Modern* (Ithaca: Cornell University Press, 1947), 21–22.
2. "Symposium," *Center Journal* 1, 3 (Summer 1982): 44–45.
3. 381 U.S. 479 (1965).
4. *Eisenstadt v. Baird*, 405 U.S. 438 (1972).
5. 410 U.S. 113 (1973).
6. *Loving v. Virginia*, 388 U.S., 1, 12.
7. 434 U.S. 374 (1978).
8. Ibid., 383, with a reference back to *Loving v. Virginia*.
9. Ibid., 386.
10. 330 U.S. 1.

14

Political Choice and Catholic Conscience

"Politique d'abord—politics first of all!'' was the slogan of Charles Maurras, an avowed atheist and French ultranationalist in the first half of this century. That slogan is almost unknown in this country, but it is the unspoken assumption of millions of Americans, including a number of Catholic politicians who don't speak a word of French and have never heard of Charles Maurras. When it comes to the crunch, however, they regularly subordinate the dictates of Catholic conscience to the demand of politics.

On the other hand, one cannot say—and I certainly do not mean to imply—that the Catholic conscience requires that all of its dictates be translated into civil and criminal law. In Catholic thought, the relationship between conscience and political decision making is considerably more nuanced than that.

Let me begin with the view on this subject of Francisco Suarez, S.J., in his great treatise, *De legibus* (*On Laws*). Suarez was not the greatest or most authoritative theologian who ever lived, but I chose him for three reasons. One is that I have read Suarez, and there are many and possibly better theologians whom I have not read. Besides, he died one year after William Shakespeare, and so clearly is not a wild-eyed post–Vatican II radical. Finally, and most important, he expounds an understanding of the nature and goals of the state that can be traced back to St. Thomas Aquinas.

Prior to Aquinas, the common opinion of the Fathers of the Church

Delivered at Wethersfield Institute conference (1992); published in *When Conscience and Politics Meet* (1993)

was that the state and its coercive power are consequences of original
sin. Had the original Paradise lasted, the state would not have been
necessary, because men would have behaved morally without needing
laws and criminal sanctions. Aquinas took over Aristotle's thesis that
man is by nature a social animal and that the state (the *polis* in Aristotle's terminology) is a necessary consequence of man's social nature. In
Thomistic theory, the state is not a mere repressor of evil, and its authority does not consist solely in its power to coerce. The state would
have been necessary even among uncorrupted and wholly good people,
because even they, too, could disagree about the best way to achieve
good ends. They would therefore need authority as a directive principle
guiding them toward the goals of the community. For St. Thomas, therefore, the state is a natural community, without which a fully human life
is not possible, and its authority is a natural human good.

One can say that Aquinas brought the idea of the state into medieval
Catholic thought. Slowly, ever so slowly, this idea shifted the focus of
discussion from the relationship of the temporal and spiritual jurisdic-
tions within a single, unified *res publica Christiana* to the relationship
between the state and the Church. Even Suarez, who inherited the Thomistic notion of the state as a natural entity and who wrote five hundred
and more years after Aquinas, had not yet fully broken away from the
res publica Christiana and the subordination of the state to the
Church—but that is not my reason for citing him here.

According to Suarez, the state is an institution of the natural order,
and is not of its nature directed to man's supernatural and eternal end,
but only to his temporal happiness, his welfare in this life. Even in this
life, the state does not per se look to the spiritual welfare of men, and
consequently the state cannot make laws disposing of or regulating spiritual matters—those are the domain of the Church. Nor is even the
natural welfare of individual men as individuals the proper end of the
state. The natural and proper function of the state is to provide for the
secular well-being of the civil community, that is to say, for its temporal
common good. The welfare of individuals concerns the state only insofar as they are members of that community.[1]

As the goal of the state and its government is limited to the temporal
common good of the political community, so is its power to make laws.
So also, therefore, is the area of political decision making limited. That,
therefore, is the arena in which the Catholic conscience, like the conscience of any other group of citizens, has its proper field of political
action. The Catholic conscience looks to the state and its lawmaking
power to legislate morality only insofar as a public morality is a compo-
nent element of the temporal common good of the whole community.

This is the position that the Second Vatican Council took in its Declaration on Religious Freedom. "The common welfare of society," it said, "consists in the entirety of those conditions of social life under which men enjoy the possibility of achieving their own perfection in a certain fullness of measure and also with some relative ease."[2] According to the Council, it is up to men to achieve their own perfection, i.e., their physical, mental, and spiritual development. The role of the state is to promote those conditions of social life that facilitate, and do not impede, that development. The main thrust of the Declaration is that among those conditions is religious freedom.

In promoting the common good, therefore, the Declaration explains:

> Government is not to act in an arbitrary fashion or in an unfair spirit of partisanship. Its action is to be controlled by juridical norms which are in conformity with the objective moral order. These norms arise out of the need for effective safeguard of the rights of all citizens and for peaceful settlement of conflicts of rights. They flow from the need for an adequate care of genuine public peace, which comes about when men live together in good order and in true justice. They come finally, out of the need for a proper guardianship of public morality. These matters constitute the basic component of the common welfare; they are what is meant by public order. For the rest, the usages of society are to be the usages of freedom in their full range.[3]

We can thus say that Vatican II supported the principle of limited government, but that it recognized a common social good and an objective moral order to which the state's juridical norms should conform. In this it was in harmony with the American legal tradition. The Preamble to the U.S. Constitution states the purposes for which the American people have framed their Constitution: "We the People of the United States, in Order to form a more perfect Union, establish Justice, insure domestic Tranquility, provide for the common defense, promote the general Welfare, and secure the Blessings of Liberty to ourselves and our Posterity, do ordain and establish this Constitution for the United States of America." Justice, domestic tranquility, common defense, general welfare, and liberty are moral as well as political goals, and are elements of the common good of the United States.

Broad as those terms are, however, they state the purpose of a federal constitution, which establishes a national government with limited powers, and assumes the existence of the several states of the Union, with their own powers derived from their state citizens. Among these state powers is what is called the police power. Various state courts over the years have defined this power as "the function of that branch of the administrative machinery of government which is charged with the preservation of public order and tranquility, the promotion of the public health, safety, and morals, and the prevention, detection, and punishment of crimes," and as "the power vested in the legislature to make, ordain, and establish all manner of wholesome and reasonable laws, statutes, and ordinances, either with penalties or without, not repugnant to the constitution, as they shall judge to be for the good and welfare of the commonwealth, and of the subjects of the same."[4] These definitions assume that, within the limits set by the state and federal constitutions, state governments are empowered to legislate and administer for the public health, safety, welfare, and morals.

If governments may act for these ends, it must be possible for the people to discuss and debate both the ends and the means to them, and to arrive at decisions in public law and policy to effectuate them, through the procedures of democratic politics. But this proposition is more and more called into question by the radically individualist and secularist view that has become the liberal orthodoxy of the opinion-making sectors of this country. One of the more extreme examples of this orthodoxy is H. Tristam Engelhardt's *The Foundations of Bioethics*,[5] in which he argues that there is no substantive moral standard of any kind that can be the basis of a public morality in a pluralistic society, because there is no such standard to which all members of the society can agree on either religious or rational grounds. The only possible basis for our common life in American society, he says, is a set of procedures to which all of us can agree as the necessary condition of our living together in peace. Those procedures become a binding moral commitment for each of us, precisely because we have agreed to them: "The moral world can be fashioned through free will, even if not on the basis of sound rational arguments with moral content."[6]

But then it turns out that there are necessary exceptions to what we can agree to. Even if we have agreed, for example, to make decisions by majority vote, some issues may not be decided by majority, not even by majorities of two-thirds or three-fourths, "unless *all* can be presumed to have agreed in advance to such procedures." But that is to say that there are substantive exceptions to the procedures:

One might think here of individuals wishing to acquire contraceptives, have abortions, take hallucinogens, or end their own lives. Laws forbidding such, even if enacted by a majority of three-fourths of the populace, are not simply of dubious authority, but may properly be seen to be attempts to use unconsented-to force against the innocent.[7]

On those terms, however, why are there any limits to the exceptions that must be made, if not only the procedures but also their results must have universal consent? One might think here of individuals wishing to acquire several wives or husbands at the same time, to have sexual relations with pubescent adolescents (who are supposed to be old enough to have abortions without notifying their parents), to engage in sadomasochism, or to practice ritual human sacrifice with willing victims, if such can be found. Or why is smoking cigarettes in public not included in the list of things that not everyone has consented to ban? One might also want to discuss whether abortion is not a use of unconsented-to force against the innocent, and why that is taken to be a closed question that may not legitimately be raised in a pluralistic society.

But let that pass. The point to be emphasized here is that every such effort to persuade us to accept a purely procedural and substantively neutral model of civil society, in which no particular notion of human good is permitted to prevail at the public level, is a flim-flam and a confidence game. It is designed to lure us into agreeing to a highly individualistic and secularist liberal agenda, which has its own substantive content. For there is no such thing as a society that is simply neutral on all questions of substantive human good. Yet those questions are what we mean by moral issues.

It does not follow that all questions of human good and morality belong in the public domain. All nontotalitarian societies draw a line between private and public moral issues, a boundary between those areas of life that are left to private choice and those that are subject to public regulation. But where that line should be drawn is itself a matter for public decision because, to safeguard the realm of private decision, there must be laws that define and protect it.

Furthermore, the public decision to protect areas of conduct regarded as private can and does vary with time and circumstance. In New York today people may legally appear naked on the stage, but the people in the audience may not smoke while looking at them. There was a time within living memory when the reverse was true. Drawing the line therefore is a political issue and one that inevitably will often have to be argued in moral terms.

To hold otherwise would be to give every group and even every individual the power to veto any public policy that embodies some conception of what human beings are and what is good for them. It would therefore constantly subordinate any understanding of the common good of society to the will of dissenters. In saying this I am not proposing a Catholic, Christian, Judeo-Christian, or any other religious orthodoxy for the pluralistic society of this country. I am only saying that political issues at some point or other raise moral questions that must be answered in the light of some conception of human nature, its basic needs, and its common social welfare. If there is nothing we can agree on about human good, then we cannot act for the welfare of our community.

If we have a welfare state, do we not need to come to some agreement on what we mean by welfare? If we take the family as an object of public policy because of its importance to society, do we not have to define the family and decide what helps or hinders it? If we wish to promote public health, must we not decide whether it ranks above or below sexual gratification (the issue that is just below the surface in the current controversy over how to respond to the spread of AIDS)? These and a host of other questions are ones that even a pluralistic society must answer, and it cannot answer them all by leaving them to private consciences.

A country's laws and public policies necessarily reflect the conscience of the people, either of the people as a whole or of the dominant element among them. In a society such as ours, which is becoming steadily more pluralistic, the common conscience is shrinking or even crumbling, and public decisions based on it are becoming more difficult to arrive at. Yet decisions must be arrived at. They cannot all be left to the individual and his private choice, because so many of them involve a view, not only of what is good for the individual, but of what is good for the community of which he is a part.

Whatever may be the grimy reality of politics, it is in principle a process by which a community comes to decisions about action for its common good. Sometimes, however, it is feared that the issues thus raised are too explosive for the political process to handle. The U.S. Supreme Court has occasionally moved in and tried to take explosively divisive issues out of the political process, most notably in *Dred Scott v. Sandford* in 1857 and *Roe v. Wade* in 1973. Such efforts often fail, however, because they do not resolve the issue in a way that both sides can accept, however reluctantly, but simply decree the victory of one side over the other. Deeply divisive issues are seldom fully resolved, but they can be brought to partial resolutions through the normal political process, and the Court would be wise to let it function. The battle over the issues will continue, but it will be a legal and nonviolent political contest in which people can learn to live with the temporary results, while hoping to achieve better ones at a later date.

Politics in a secular democratic state is concerned with the content of the temporal good of the community in this world, and with the means of achieving it. Both the content and the means are subject to political dispute and debate. It does not follow that only secularists may take part in the debate, or that Catholics must check their consciences at the door when entering the public forum, or that we must obey the secularists when they shout: "Sit down, shut up, and let us run the country!" Catholics, like all other citizens, have a right to bring their view of the public welfare, informed by their conscience, to bear on questions that are properly issues of public policy. The state is separate from the Church, but it is not separate from the consciences that churches form.

A recent example of secularist arrogance appeared, not in the *New York Times,* where you might expect it, but in an editorial in the *San Antonio* [Texas] *Express-News* on August 30, 1992: "This nation's goodness is deep-rooted and only superficially religion-based." That statement is in itself a very superficial judgment. It is true, and zealots should never forget it, that we can seldom argue directly from religious premises to concrete public-policy conclusions as if those conclusions were the manifest will of God. But it is equally naive to ignore the social reality that a people's laws reflect their moral convictions, that these in turn reflect their beliefs about the nature of man and of the world we live in, and that such beliefs historically have been rooted in their religion or religions. It is worth mentioning that the religions of this country, despite their multiplicity, have generally shared a common biblical moral tradition.

A universe created by a personal and loving God and populated by persons made in the image and likeness of God is a vastly different place from a universe that has evolved through the blind operation of the forces of matter and is populated by humanoids who, far from being a little less than the angels (for there are no angels), are only a cut above the apes. Whichever of these two views you hold will not tell you whether we should or should not reduce the capital gains tax. But it will have a profound effect on how you think about deeper and much more important issues.

As we have noted previously, James Fitzjames Stephen saw this clearly in England as long ago as 1873. Stephen lost his faith in Christianity altogether, but he nonetheless said that if belief in a personal God and a future life should disappear, "there will be an end of what is commonly called religion, and it will be necessary to reconstruct morals from end to end."[8] The reason he gave was this:

If these beliefs are mere dreams, life is a very much poorer and pettier thing; men are beings of much less importance; trouble, danger, and physical pain are much greater evils, and the prudence of virtue is much more questionable than has hitherto been supposed to be the case. If men follow the advice so often pressed upon them, to cease to think of these subjects otherwise than as insoluble riddles, all the existing conceptions of morality will have to be changed, all social tendencies will be weakened. Merely personal inclinations will be greatly strengthened.[9]

In particular, said Stephen, "The value which is set upon human life, especially upon the lives of the sick, the wretched, and superfluous children would at once appear to be exaggerated. Lawyers would have occasion to reconsider the law of murder, and especially the law of infanticide."[10] We have reached that point today, and we must give Stephen credit for having foreseen, well over a century ago, what so many people who call themselves Christians and Catholics refuse to see at this late date.

It is, of course, irrelevant, although secularists will rush to remind us of it, that some Catholics are worse in their personal lives than high-minded agnostics. It is also a sublime missing of the point to say that we live in a pluralistic society and must therefore settle for the lowest common denominator in our public morality. The lowest denominator is not common. To take the most obvious examples, we do not all hold a secularist view of the value of human life, of the meaning and importance of sex, and of the nature of marriage and the family. It is begging the question to assume that because we disagree on them, therefore these are all subjects of merely personal choice, of little or no significance to society and its common good.

On the contrary, these matters are properly in the public forum and are subject to public debate and possible regulation. A Catholic understanding of them has as much right as any other to present itself and to influence public decisions concerning them. I do not say that Catholics have a right to force others to accept their faith. Nor do I suggest that sound public policies in regard to these matters depend on a general acceptance of Catholic theology. I do say that Catholics may and should vigorously present their understanding of these and other topics of vital concern to the whole community's general welfare.

If we do that, without allowing ourselves to be brow-beaten into silence, we may reasonably hope to find areas of agreement with many of our fellow citizens who are not of our faith, and even with some who have no religious faith. After all, there are agnostics and atheists who feel that one-and-a-half million abortions a year are too many, that easy divorce has seriously undesirable social effects, that the sexual preachments of Madonna and other heralds of the new morality do not furnish a sound basis for public education, and that homosexuality is not really on a par with heterosexuality when we legislate concerning marriage.

At this point, I should proceed to make some important distinctions about what Catholics (or any other group) should try to accomplish through political and legal action. As Edmund Burke put it, it is no inconsiderable part of wisdom to know how much of an evil ought to be tolerated. But, precisely because it requires so much practical, prudential wisdom to know when and how to act against evils, and when to refrain from action, discussing this aspect of the subject would take more time and space than I have at my present disposal. I shall merely note that a full discussion of political choice and Catholic conscience would require taking up that topic, and let it rest there. My main, and indeed only, point has been that while the authority of the state is limited to the secular, temporal good of the civil community, even in that area politics is not supreme and a law unto itself. It is subject to the moral judgment of the citizens, including those who believe in the God in which this nation allegedly trusts.

Notes

1. For Suarez's own words, see the footnotes in an article, ''Subordination of the State to the Church in Suarez,'' that I had published in *Theological Studies* 12 (1951): 354–64.

2. Sect. 6, *The Documents of Vatican II*, ed. Abbott and Gallagher (New York: Guild Press, America Press, Association Press, 1966), p. 683.

3. Sect. 7, ibid., pp. 686–87.

4. *Black's Law Dictionary* (St. Paul, Minn.: West Publishing Co., 1951), p. 1316, col. 1, and p. 1317, col. 1.

5. New York: Oxford University Press, 1986.

6. Ibid., p. 42.

7. Ibid., p. 46.

8. *Liberty, Equality, Fraternity* (reprinted by the Cambridge University Press in 1967), p. 39.

9. Ibid., p. 98.

10. Ibid., p. 48.

Index

159

About the Author

Francis Canavan is a professor emeritus of political science at Fordham University. He is the author of three books on the political thought of Edmund Burke and one on freedom of expression and edited *The Ethical Dimension of Political Life*, a festschrift for the late John H. Hallowell.